European Ui

2011–2012

This edition updated by Sonia Morano-Foadi and Johanna Diekmann

Routledge
Taylor & Francis Group

LONDON AND NEW YORK

Eighth edition published 2011
by Routledge
2 Park Square, Milton Park, Abingdon, Oxon, OX14 4RN

Simultaneously published in the USA and Canada
by Routledge
270 Madison Avenue, New York, NY 10016

Routledge is an imprint of the Taylor & Francis Group, an informa business

© 2006, 2009, 2010, 2011 Routledge

Previous editions published by Cavendish Publishing Limited
First edition   1997
Second edition   1999
Third edition   2002
Fourth edition   2004

Previous editions published by Routledge
Fifth edition   2006
Sixth edition   2009
Seventh edition   2010

Typeset in Rotis by RefineCatch Limited, Bungay, Suffolk
Printed and bound in Great Britain by TJ International Ltd, Padstow, Cornwall

British Library Cataloguing in Publication Data
A catalogue record for this book is available from the British Library

Library of Congress Cataloging in Publication Data
A catalog record for this book has been requested

ISBN13: 978-0-415-61868-7 (pbk)
ISBN13: 978-0-203-82836-6 (eBook)

Contents

Table of Cases

Table of Statutes

Table of Statutory Instruments

Table of European Legislation

How to use this book

Welcome to this new edition of Routledge European Union Law Lawcards. In response to student feedback, we've added some new features to these new editions to give you all the support and preparation you need in order to face your law exams with confidence.

Inside this book you will find:

■ NEW tables of cases and statutes for ease of reference

■ Revision Checklists

We've summarised the key topics you will need to know for your law exams and broken them down into a handy revision checklist. Check them out at the beginning of each chapter, then after you have the chapter down, revisit the checklist and tick each topic off as you gain knowledge and confidence.

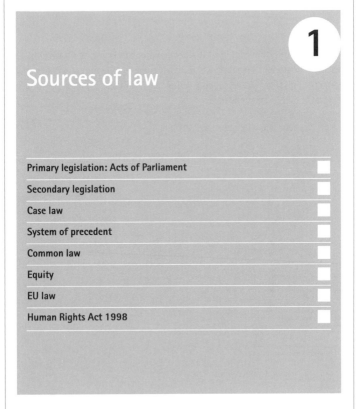

1

Sources of law

Primary legislation: Acts of Parliament ☐

Secondary legislation ☐

Case law ☐

System of precedent ☐

Common law ☐

Equity ☐

EU law ☐

Human Rights Act 1998 ☐

■ Key Cases

We've identified the key cases that are most likely to come up in exams. To help you to ensure that you can cite cases with ease, we've included a brief account of the case and judgment for a quick aide-memoire.

HENDY LENNOX v GRAHAME PUTTICK [1984]

Basic facts

Diesel engines were supplied, subject to a *Romalpa* clause, then fitted to generators. Each engine had a serial number. When the buyer became insolvent the seller sought to recover one engine. The Receiver argued that the process of fitting the engine to the generator passed property to the buyer. The court disagreed and allowed the seller to recover the still identifiable engine despite the fact that some hours of work would be required to disconnect it.

Relevance

If the property remains identifiable and is not irredeemably changed by the manufacturing process, a *Romalpa* clause may be viable.

Companion Website

At the end of each chapter you will be prompted to visit the Routledge Lawcards companion website, where you can test your understanding online with specially prepared multiple-choice questions, as well as revise the key terms with our online glossary.

You should now be confident that you would be able to tick all of the boxes on the checklist at the beginning of this chapter. To check your knowledge of Sources of law, why not visit the companion website and take the Multiple Choice Question test. Check your understanding of the terms and vocabulary used in this chapter with the flashcard glossary.

Exam Practice

Once you've acquired the basic knowledge, you'll want to put it to the test. The Routledge Questions and Answers provides examples of the kinds of questions that you will face in your exams, together with suggested answer plans and a fully-worked model answer. We've included one example free at the end of this book to help you put your technique and understanding into practice.

QUESTION 1

What are the main sources of law today?

Answer plan

This is, apparently, a very straightforward question, but the temptation is to ignore the European Community (EU) as a source of law and to over-emphasise custom as a source. The following structure does not make these mistakes:

- in the contemporary situation, it would not be improper to start with the EU as a source of UK law;
- then attention should be moved on to domestic sources of law: statute and common law;
- the increased use of delegated legislation should be emphasised;
- custom should be referred to, but its extremely limited operation must be emphasised.

ANSWER

European law

Since the UK joined the European Economic Community (EEC), now the EU, it has progressively but effectively passed the power to create laws which are operative in this country to the wider European institutions. The UK is now subject to Community law, not just as a direct consequence of the various treaties of accession passed by the UK Parliament, but increasingly, it is subject to the secondary legislation generated by the various institutions of the EU.

The establishment of the European Communities and European Union and sources of law

Explain why the European Communities were established
and how the European Union has developed ◼

Explain the key features of the Treaties establishing the European
Communities and the European Union and the content of the
amending Treaties ◼

Outline the main features of the Treaty of Lisbon ◼

Identify and discuss the four main sources of EU law ◼

Discuss the requirements that new EU Legislation must satisfy in
order to be legally valid ◼

SOURCES OF LAW

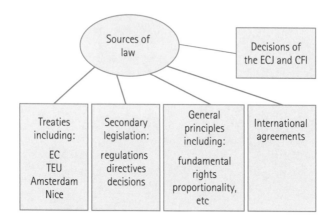

There are four sources of EU law:

- ▣ law enacted by Member States which are the founding Treaties (primary legislation) and law enacted by the EU (secondary legislation);

- ▣ general principles of law recognised by the Court of Justice (CJ) [formerly European Court of Justice (ECJ)];

- ▣ international agreements with non-Member States;

- ▣ decisions of the Court of Justice and the General Court [formerly Court of First Instance (CFI)].

PRIMARY LEGISLATION

One of the main characteristics of the EU legal order is that it is based on a written constitution made up of the constitutive Treaties as follows:

ECSC Treaty (1951)
EC Treaty (1957)
EURATOM Treaty (1957)
Convention Relating to Certain Institutions Common to European
  Communities (1957)

Merger Treaty (1965)
First and Second Budgetary Treaties (1970 and 1975)
Treaties of Accession (1972, 1979, 1985, 1994, 2003 and 2005)
Single European Act (1986)
Treaty on European Union (1992)
Treaty of Amsterdam (1997)
Treaty of Nice (2001)
Treaty of Lisbon (2007)

European Coal and Steel Community Treaty (ECSC)

Established by the Treaty of Paris in 1951, the purpose of the European Coal and Steel Community (ECSC) was to create a common market for coal and steel products.

The ECSC Treaty was the first of the constitutive Treaties. It exhibited a functionalist approach to integration, attempting to integrate economies sector by sector. A criticism of this approach is that it was an unnatural operation, as the integrated sector retained indissoluble links with other sectors of the economy which still had their national character. Its justification was that it was a first step, to be followed by integration of other sectors of the economy, toward the eventual integration of the whole economy.

An innovative feature of the ECSC Treaty was the creation of four supra-national institutions:

1 Council of Ministers – representing the Member States;
2 High Authority – intended as a supra-national executive, consisting of independent individuals rather than government representatives, empowered to take legally binding decisions and to procure funds, fix maximum and minimum prices for certain products and fine businesses in breach of competition rules;
3 Assembly – a parliament composed of delegates appointed by respective parliaments of the Member States;
4 Court of Justice – intended to review the legality of the Acts of the High Authority or, in some cases, businesses.

(Note: The ECSC lapsed in July 2002.)

3

European Atomic Energy Community Treaty (EURATOM)

Established by the Treaty of Rome in 1957, the purpose of EURATOM was to create a specialist market for atomic energy and distribute it through the Community, and to develop nuclear energy and sell surplus to non-Community States.

EURATOM had its own Commission (which was the equivalent of the ECSC's High Authority) and Council of Ministers, but shared an Assembly and Court of Justice with the ECSC and European Economic Community. EURATOM was another example of sectoral, or functional, integration.

European Economic Community Treaty (the European Community after the TEU)

The European Economic Community was established by a separate Treaty of Rome in 1957, and its name was amended by the Treaty on European Union (TEU). Its aim, as stated in the Preamble, was 'to lay the foundations of an ever closer union among the peoples of Europe'.

MEMBERSHIP

The original EEC was formed by six Member States: Belgium, France, (West) Germany, Italy, Luxembourg and the Netherlands. Since then the EEC (subsequently renamed EC) has expanded to include a further 21 countries: Denmark, Ireland and the UK (in 1973), Greece (1981), Portugal and Spain (1986), Austria, Finland and Sweden (1995), Cyprus, Czech Republic, Estonia, Hungary, Latvia, Lithuania, Malta, Poland, Slovakia and Slovenia (2004), Bulgaria and Romania (2007). Negotiations continue with Turkey.

The EEC had its own separate Commission and Council of Ministers but it shared an Assembly and Court of Justice with EURATOM and the ECSC.

The Treaty of Rome embodied a very different approach to integration from that of the ECSC and EURATOM Treaties. Whereas the latter attempted to integrate sector by sector, the EEC Treaty concentrated on types of activity rather than particular industries (with the exception of agriculture and transport), and aimed to ensure the effective functioning of the market together with free and fair competition. Another characteristic of the Treaty of Rome was that it laid down general principles, leaving it to the institutions to enact in detail. Policy making and regulation were also left to the institutions. Timetables were laid down for the elimination of both mutual trade barriers and the common external tariff. Through these methods, the founders hoped to achieve economic integration, which was intended to be the forerunner of political integration. The Treaty was intended as a first step, to be followed by later Treaties which would build on the progress made.

Merger Treaty

The three different Communities had created three different sets of institutions, although they shared the same Assembly and Court of Justice. It became inconvenient to have three different sets of institutions, so a Merger Treaty came into force in 1967. The three Communities themselves did not merge, but the High Authority and two Commissions merged to form a single Commission, and the three Councils merged to form a single Council. Hartley, in *Foundations of European Community Law*, 5th edn, 2003, uses the analogy of three commercial companies with the same shareholders and same board of directors. In law, there are three legal persons; in reality, there is one.

The most important features of the Merger Treaty have been incorporated into the EC Treaty by the Treaty on European Union.

Single European Act (SEA)

Signed in 1986, the SEA was the first major amendment to the EC Treaty. It came about as a result of pressure for increased union and concern over increased competition from North America and the Far East. A major aim of the SEA was to speed up the decision making process through greater use of qualified majority voting, a system of weighted voting whereby Member States with larger populations receive more votes in the Council of Ministers than those States with smaller populations.

The SEA saw a widening of the process of European integration. This is illustrated by powers given to the EC in new areas. Whilst the original Treaty of Rome was principally concerned with integration of types of economic activity, the SEA granted powers to the EC for the co-ordination of economic and monetary policy and foreign policy. Both areas had been left out of the original Treaty. Other new areas included: social policy; powers to create a regional policy called 'economic and social cohesion'; environmental policy; and co-operation in research and technological development. The process of European integration could also be said to have been deepened, as well as widened, by the SEA.

The greater use of qualified majority voting meant that Member States could be out-voted and bound against their will. This represented a significant transfer of sovereignty from Member States to the European Community. Greater powers were also given to the European Parliament, an institution which is not under national control. The Commission, which is also outside national control, was given a central role in ensuring that the internal market was set up on time.

The major amendments were as follows:

- inauguration of the internal market programme for completion by 31 December 1992;

- introduction of qualified majority voting in the Council of Ministers for enactment of measures where they have as their object 'the establishment and functioning of the internal market';

- change in implementing powers of the Commission;

- creation of a co-operation procedure for enhanced consultative participation of the European Parliament in the legislative process;

- power of veto given to the European Parliament over the accession of new Member States and over the conclusion of agreements with associate States;

- recognition of the European Council as a formal organ of the European Community;

- authority granted to the Council of Ministers to create the Court of First Instance;

- co-operation in the field of foreign policy through European political co-operation;

- co-operation in economic and monetary policy;

- common policy for the environment;

- co-operation in research and technological development;

■ measures to ensure the economic and social cohesion of the Community;

■ harmonisation in the fields of health, safety, consumer protection, academic, professional and vocational qualifications, public procurement, VAT and Excise duties and frontier controls.

Treaty on European Union (TEU)

The next amendment to the EC Treaty was the Maastricht Treaty (officially known as the Treaty on European Union). The TEU created a European Union with three pillars: European Community, Common Foreign and Security Policy, and Justice and Home Affairs Policy.

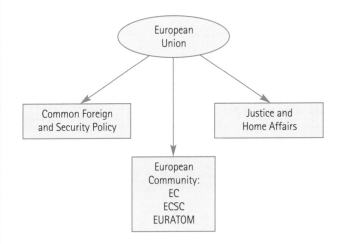

General principles

The Treaty on European Union has provisions on three matters of constitutional importance: human rights, subsidiarity and citizenship:

■ Article 6 of the TEU enshrines the existing practice that fundamental human rights are to be a general principle of Community law;

■ the principle of subsidiarity was introduced into EC law, in matters relating to the environment, by the SEA. It was made a general principle of EC law by virtue of the TEU. Article 5 TEU (formerly Art 5 of the EC Treaty) provides that, in matters which are not within the Community's exclusive competence, the Community will only take action if the scale of the proposed action means that it can be better achieved by the Community;

- every national of a Member State is to become a citizen of the European Union (Art 20 TFEU and formerly Art 17 of the EC Treaty).

Economic and monetary union

The Treaty sets out the procedure and timetable for creating economic and monetary union (EMU).

Other changes

The TEU introduced a number of other changes, including:

- establishment of a Committee of Regions;

- Court of Auditors becomes a Community institution;

- greater powers for the European Parliament, with the introduction of a new legislative procedure (co-decision).

Treaty of Amsterdam (ToA)

The Treaty of Amsterdam, which came into force in May 1999, was a consolidation, rather than an extension, of Community powers. It was also intended to prepare the Community for an expansion in membership, with the inclusion of Central and Eastern European States. A further aim was to make the European Union seem less remote to the citizens of Europe.

Common provisions

A principle of openness was added to the Treaty, so that decisions are taken 'as openly as possible' and as closely as possible to the citizen. Article 6 of the TEU, which enshrined the principle of fundamental human rights in the Treaty, has been amended. If the Council of the European Union finds a 'persistent and serious breach' by a Member State of the principles of fundamental human rights, the Council may suspend some of the State's rights under the Treaty, including voting rights.

Other changes

Other changes introduced by the ToA include the following:

- Much of the third pillar of the European Union, the Justice and Home Affairs pillar, is incorporated into the EC Treaty. The third pillar now covers

Police and Judicial Co-operation in Criminal Matters (PJCC). The body of law, *acquis communautaire*, created by the Schengen Treaty 1985, which gradually abolishes border checks, is brought within the EU. The UK and Ireland are not bound by the Schengen *acquis* but can opt in whenever they wish to do so. Denmark has a partial opt-out from the Schengen *acquis*.

▨ There is an attempt to simplify the EC Treaty, which includes renumbering.

▨ The Community is given new tasks. The promotion of equality between men and women, protection and improvement of the environment, a high degree of competitiveness and 'sustainable' economic development are expressly stated to be Community goals.

▨ The Luxembourg Accords, which grant a Member State a right of veto if a decision affects one of its vital national interests, are enshrined in the Treaty. The right of veto had previously been a constitutional convention.

▨ New powers are given in the field of non-discrimination. The Community now has competence to combat discrimination in the fields of sex, racial or ethnic origin, religion or belief, disability, age and sexual orientation.

▨ A new title on employment has been added to the EC Treaty. Measures taken under this section are intended to support and complement national measures. The measures are confined to being 'soft law', ie, they are not legally binding.

▨ The co-decision procedure is amended and extended to new areas, thereby strengthening the role of the European Parliament.

▨ The Committee of Regions has the right to be consulted in a wider number of areas.

▨ The European Parliament is given the right to consult the Committee of Regions and the Economic and Social Committee, as well as the Council and the Parliament.

▨ The Community is given legislative power to combat fraud.

▨ A principle of flexibility is enshrined in the Treaty. This allows groups of Member States to integrate and co-operate further on specific issues when there is no agreement amongst all the Member States about the need for further integration or co-operation. It is possible for these groups of States to make use of the procedures, institutions and mechanisms laid down in the Treaty.

Treaty of Nice

In February 2001 the Treaty of Nice was signed. After ratification, it came into force in February 2003. The main points are as follows:

- ▢ Reweighting of votes during qualified majority voting (QMV) procedures in the Council of Ministers. More power is given to the larger nations: the UK, Germany, France, Italy and Spain.

- ▢ Use of QMV in the Council of Ministers is increased for reasons of speed and efficiency. Approximately 39 new policy areas no longer require a unanimous vote.

- ▢ An unanimous vote will still be required for legislation regarding taxation, social security, immigration, movement of professionals and foreign trade in culture.

- ▢ Groups of eight or more countries will be able to pursue further integration independently under a new 'reinforced co-operation' procedure.

The Charter of Fundamental Rights

The Charter of Fundamental Rights (2007/C 303/01) of the European Union was drafted by a Convention composed of representatives of the governments of the EU's Member States, the Commission, the European Parliament and national parliaments. In 2000 the Charter of Fundamental Rights was approved by the European Council. The document consists of 50 articles on a range of issues. It is essentially a consolidation of rights derived from a variety of pre-existing documents, such as the European Convention on Human Rights and the Community Charter of the Fundamental Social Rights of Workers (1989). Some of the key rights and freedoms in the Charter are right to life (Art 2); prohibition of torture and inhuman or degrading treatment or punishment (Art 4); prohibition of slavery and forced labour (Art 5); respect for private and family life (Art 7); freedom of thought, conscience and religion (Art 10); equality between men and women (Art 23); freedom of movement and of residence (Art 45).

Article 51 of the Charter states that its provisions are 'addressed to the institutions and bodies of the Union . . . and to the Member States only when they are implementing Union law'. This is narrower in scope than the case law which applies to Member States when they are implementing EU law (*Wachauf* [1989]) and when they are derogating from EU law: *ERT* [1991]; *Familiapress* [1997].

The legal status of this Charter was not entirely clear – the Nice declaration specifically refrained from giving it binding legal force. However, this did not mean that its provisions had no relevance whatsoever. It had been an authoritative statement of the rights considered to be fundamental in the Union. In several cases from 2001 onwards various Advocates-General have referred to it during proceedings in cases pending before the ECJ (see Chapter 3). In *BECTU* (2001), for example, Advocate-General Tizzano said:

> . . . in proceedings concerned with the nature and scope of a funda-
> mental right, the relevant statements of the Charter cannot be
> ignored; in particular, we cannot ignore its clear purpose of serving,
> where its provisions so allow, as a substantive point of reference for
> all those involved – Member States, institutions, natural and legal
> persons – in the Community context.

Now with the entering into force of the Lisbon Treaty under Art 6(1) TEU the Charter is, though not part of the Treaty, given 'the same legal value as the Treaties'. Under the new Treaty, it is therefore legally binding on the institutions of the Union and on the Member States, with the limitation that the latter have to be 'implementing Union law'.

The European Convention

At the European Council summit meeting in Laeken, Belgium, in December 2001, it was agreed that the EU needed a constitution. Officially, the idea of a Constitution is to make the principles and objectives of the EU more accessible to its citizens. Cynics suggest that it is more than this – it is paving the way for a 'federal' Europe – a 'United States of Europe'.

Notwithstanding the political arguments, a body named the European Convention was set up in spring 2002 to start work on drafting a Constitution. The Convention team comprised 105 people representing the existing and prospective EU Member States and their Parliaments, the European Parliament and the Commission. It was chaired by the former French president Valéry Giscard d'Estaing. The Convention produced its final draft Constitution in May 2003. Key proposals include:

- An elected president (elected by EU leaders that is) to serve as a figurehead for a period of 2½–5 years.

- A foreign minister to conduct a common foreign policy (including defence and security policy).

- The Commission would be capped at 15 full members.

- The Charter of Fundamental Rights to become legally binding.

- The various Treaties on which the EU is based would be fully consolidated into one document.

- Existing Member States would be allowed to negotiate withdrawal from the EU (no State has ever withdrawn).

The draft Constitution was signed by the heads of State of the 25 Member States in October 2004. The next stage in bringing the Constitution into effect was ratification, either by the EU's Member States' parliaments or their citizens in a referendum. All of the Member States were required to vote in favour. The ratification process had started in a relatively uncontroversial fashion. By the end of May 2005, the parliaments of eight countries (Austria, Germany, Greece, Hungary, Italy, Lithuania, Slovakia and Slovenia) had voted in favour. A successful referendum was held in Spain in February 2005 (with nearly 77 per cent voting yes).

However, the ratification process was thrown into turmoil and confusion when the French voted '*non*' in a referendum at the end of May 2005 (with nearly 55 per cent voting against the Constitution from a very high turnout, over 69 per cent of the electorate), followed a few days later by an even more emphatic '*nee*' in the Netherlands (nearly 62 per cent voting against).

Treaty of Lisbon

The Constitutional Treaty was subsequently abandoned and an alternative Treaty was negotiated called the Treaty of Lisbon, which was signed by 27 heads of state on 13 December 2007. The Irish voters approved the Treaty of Lisbon in a second referendum held in October 2009. The Treaty of Lisbon entered into force on 1 December 2009.

Unlike the failed Constitution, the Treaty of Lisbon does not replace the Treaties but instead amends the EC Treaty (renamed the Treaty on the Functioning of the European Union) and the Treaty on European Union. The key innovations are as follows:

■ The term 'European Community' will merge into the European Union (there is no need to refer to the EC or the Community any longer).

■ An elected 'permanent' president (elected by the European Council by a qualified majority) for a term of two and a half years renewable once, thereby replacing the current six monthly rotating presidency, which is held by a Member State not by a person.

■ A new post of High Representative of the EU for Foreign Affairs and Security Policy who will also be one of the Commission's Vice-Presidents. It is believed that this will increase the impact, coherence and the visibility of the EU's external actions.

■ The Charter of Fundamental Rights 2000 is afforded 'the same legal value as the Treaties' and is now part of the EU's primary law. The UK has obtained a legally binding protocol providing that no court can rule that the laws, regulations or administrative provisions or practices of the UK are inconsistent with the principles laid down in the Charter of Fundamental Rights. Furthermore, that the Charter creates no new rights enforceable in the UK over and above those already existing in UK domestic law.

■ The EU has single legal personality to act in the international arena in a more coherent way.

■ The Treaty confirms the primacy of EU law over the law of Member States in line with longstanding case law.

■ The 'pillar structure' of the Union disappears and what was the third pillar ('Justice and Home Affairs', now 'Police and Judicial Cooperation in Criminal Matters') is subsumed within the Title V of the TFEU. The CJ's normal jurisdiction becomes generally applicable.

■ The Treaty provides that the Council shall act by qualified majority voting except where the Treaties provide otherwise. This means that qualified majority voting will become the normal voting system in the Council of the European Union.

- The Treaty provides that any Member State may decide to withdraw from the Union in accordance with its own constitutional requirements.

- The Treaty provides that the Union will get an extended capacity to act on freedom, security and justice.

- The Treaty provides a strengthened role for the European Parliament by extending the co-decision procedure and placing the European Parliament on a more equal footing with the Council of the European Union.

GENERAL PRINCIPLES OF EU LAW

In every legal system, the written sources of law do not provide the answer to every problem which appears before the courts. The Court of Justice (CJ) has, therefore, had to develop general principles of law to provide a foundation for judgment.

SOURCES OF GENERAL PRINCIPLES

The Treaties also provide specific justification for the development of general principles of law.

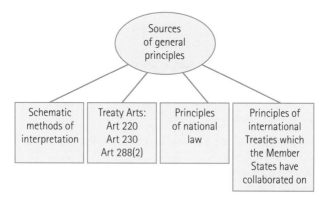

- *Article 19 TEU (formerly Article 220 TEC)*: the CJ shall ensure that in the interpretation and application of the Treaty the law is observed. This implies that 'the law' includes not only the written sources of law in the Treaty itself but also general principles created by the judiciary.

- *Article 263 TFEU (formerly Art 230 TEC)*: this lays down the grounds on which a Community act may be annulled. One of these grounds is 'infringement of this Treaty or any rule of law relating to its application'. The phrase 'any rule of law' must refer to something other than the Treaty itself.

- *Article 340(2) TFEU (formerly Art 288(2) TEC)*: this is concerned with non-contractual liability and provides that the liability of the Union is based on 'the general principles common to the laws of the Member States'.

Principles of the national laws of the Member States

The CJ has adopted principles taken from national laws of Member States. A principle need not be one of every Member State. Whatever the origin of the principle, it will be applied by the CJ as a principle of EU law, not national law.

Principles of human rights in International Treaties

The CJ, in the case of *Nold v Commission* [1974], held that the general principle of fundamental rights was also inspired by Treaties on which the Member States have collaborated or of which they are signatories.

FUNDAMENTAL HUMAN RIGHTS

Every Member State is a signatory of the European Convention on Human Rights and Fundamental Freedoms (ECHR). Art 6(2) TEU commits the EU to accession to the European Convention for the ECHR. In *Bosphorus v Ireland* [2008], the European Court of Human Rights in Strasbourg ruled that the EU system of protection of fundamental rights is equivalent to that in the ECHR and established the presumption that a state has not departed from the requirement of the Convention when it does no more than implement legal obligations flowing from its EU membership (para 156). It states that action against national measures governed by EU law would be upheld not if the measure breaches the ECHR but only if it is a 'manifested deficient'. *Chalmers, Davies and Monti* named this a 'non-aggression pact' between the CJ and the Strasbourg court (261, 2010).

The commitment of the Union to human rights is enshrined in Art 6 TEU. This constituted a recognition of the long standing practice of acceptance of fundamental human rights as a general principle of EU law, which started with the case of *Stauder v City of Ulm* [1969].

The rights which have been recognised by the CJ include:

- property rights, although these are not absolute and unqualified (*Nold v Commission* [1974]);

- religious rights (*Prais v Council* [1976]);

- right to privacy (*National Panasonic (UK) Ltd v Commission* [1979]), although this did not extend to the issue of seizing goods for the purposes of EC competition law;

- right to client-lawyer privacy (*AM and S Europe v Commission* [1982]);

- due process of law (*Musique Diffusion Française SA v Commission* [1984]);

- non-retroactivity of criminal law (*R v Kirk* [1984]);

- principle of legal review (*Heylens* [1987]).

It should be noted that the CJ has relied on general principles of fundamental rights to review the legality of acts of both the EU institutions and Member States. Member States are required to comply with fundamental rights when they are implementing EU law (*Wachauf* [1989]) and when they are derogating from EU law: *ERT* [1991]; *Familiapress* [1997].

The Treaty of Lisbon provides two significant changes in relation to Fundamental Rights: firstly, the Charter of Fundamental Rights becomes legally binding, and secondly, the new legal basis to accede to the ECHR has been encompassed in the Treaty.

The gradual recognition of fundamental rights as general principles of EU law by the Court of Justice and the legally binding effect of the Charter of Fundamental Rights of the European Union (see above) have strengthened the protection of fundamental rights within the EU.

PRINCIPLE OF EQUALITY

The TFEU (formerly EC Treaty) contains specific examples of the principle of equality, as follows:

- discrimination on grounds of sex, nationality, racial or ethnic origin, religion or belief, disability, age or sexual orientation are prohibited (Arts 18 and 19 TFEU, formerly Arts 12 and 13 TEC);

- discrimination between producers and employers in agricultural production is prohibited (Art 40 TFEU, formerly Art 34 TEC);

- discrimination between employees on grounds of sex is prohibited (Art 157 TFEU, formerly Art 141 EC).

The CJ has taken these specific examples and deduced from them a general principle of equality (*Frilli* [1972]).

The principle of equality means that persons in similar situations are not to be treated differently, unless the difference in treatment is objectively justified.

PROPORTIONALITY

This is a principle borrowed from German law. According to this principle, a public authority may not impose obligations on a citizen except to the extent that they are strictly necessary for, or proportionate to, the aim that is sought.

LEGAL CERTAINTY

Legal certainty is a part of most legal systems, but in EU law the concept has become more complex, with various sub-concepts such as non-retroactivity, vested rights and legitimate expectations. (*Kolpinghuis Nijmegen* [1986]).

Non retroactivity and 'vested rights'

The concept of vested rights is often no more than another aspect of retro-activity, but it can also refer to such matters as the rule of law and the independence of the judiciary. They are rights acquired within the society's legal framework and under due process. The idea is that, at any given time, a person should know his legal position, and rights should not be taken away by retrospective legislation.

Legitimate expectations

This is another concept which has been borrowed from German law. It was first applied in *Commission v Council* (*First Staff Salaries* case) [1973]. The Council had agreed a pay formula for Commission staff which was to last for three years. Before the three years had expired, the Council attempted to impose a new formula. It was held that the new pay scales were invalid as they infringed legitimate expectations.

LEGAL PROFESSIONAL PRIVILEGE

It was recognised in *AM and S v Commission* [1979] that confidentiality of written communications between lawyer and client was a general principle of EU law, but it was subject to two conditions. First, the communication must be for the client's defence. Second, the lawyer must be in private practice.

It was held in *National Panasonic (UK) Ltd v Commission* [1979] that, where a party was attempting to use legal professional privilege to thwart the enforcement of EU competition law, there was no violation of a right to privacy.

DUE PROCESS AND NATURAL JUSTICE

This principle has been drawn from English law and requires the making and enforcement of rules of conduct to comply with due process. For example, it was held in *Transocean Paint Association v Commission* [1974] that, where a person's interests are affected by a decision of a public authority, that person must be given the opportunity to make his view known before the decision is heard.

SECONDARY LEGISLATION

The TFEU (formerly EC Treaty) defines three types of legally binding acts:

1 regulations;
2 directives;
3 decisions.

It also includes two non-legally binding acts:

1 recommendations;
2 opinions.

REGULATIONS

Article 288 TFEU (formerly Art 249 TEC) provides that regulations have general application. They are also binding in their entirety and are directly applicable in all Member States. As to the meaning of 'direct applicability', see Chapter 2. Regulations help to ensure uniformity of law throughout the EU. They are normative in character and will apply generally or to groups of people identifiable in the abstract.

DIRECTIVES

Article 288 TFEU (formerly Art 249 TEC) provides that directives are binding 'as to the result to be achieved'. They are binding on the Member States and do not bind individuals until they have been transposed into national law. Although they are binding on the Member States, the choice of form and methods when transposing them into national law is left to the national authorities. The purpose of directives is to set a common aim for the Member States. The Member States can then use the most appropriate methods for achieving this aim in their own legal system.

It has been held by the Court of Justice (CJ) that directives may have direct effect. This is discussed in Chapter 2.

Individuals may be able to apply for compensation when they have suffered loss as a result of the incorrect transposition of a directive. This is discussed in Chapter 2.

	Regulations	Directives
Bind	People generally (everybody)	Member States
Extent to which they bind	In their entirety	Result to be achieved
Need national measures?	No	Must have implementing measures

DECISIONS

Article 288 TFEU (formerly Art 249 TEC) provides that decisions are binding on those to whom they are addressed. They can be addressed to individual Member States, corporations or private individuals. They differ from regulations, in that they personally address people as opposed to applying to people or groups of people in the abstract.

RECOMMENDATIONS AND OPINIONS

Recommendations and opinions have no binding force and are of persuasive authority only. In *Grimaldi v Fonds des Maladies Professionnelles* [1988], the CJ said that national courts are 'bound to take recommendations into consideration in deciding disputes submitted to them, in particular where they clarify the interpretation of national provisions adopted in order to implement them or where they are designed to supplement binding EEC measures'.

Problems with classification of legal acts

It was held in *Confederation Nationale des Producteurs de Fruits et Legumes v Council* [1962] that the legal classification of a legislative act will depend on its substance rather than its form. An act can be called a regulation, but if it is in substance a decision, it will be treated as such. Consequently, in *International Fruit Co NV v Commission (No 1)* [1970], what was termed a 'regulation' was, in fact, a bundle of decisions.

Article 288 TFEU (formerly Art 249 TEC) envisages distinct roles for each of the different types of legislative acts. In practice, however, there has been a blurring of the different acts. The CJ has ruled that directives and decisions may have direct effect, which makes them less distinct from regulations than one would suppose from a casual reading of Art 288 TFEU (formerly Art 249 TEC). Directives have often been very detailed when their function was to set an aim which would be fulfilled through national implementing legislation. If the directive is highly detailed, then the Member State is not left with much discretion to frame the legislation in the most appropriate way to its own legal order.

It has been found that some legislative acts are 'hybrids' and are in part a regulation and in part a decision: *NTN Toyo Bearing Co Ltd v Council* [1979], *per* AG Warner.

The list of acts contained in Art 288 TFEU (formerly Art 249 TEC) is not exhaustive. The CJ has held that other types of act are legally binding. For example, in *Les Verts v European Parliament* [1986], a decision of the Bureau of the European Parliament relating to the distribution of funds prior to the 1984 direct elections was held to be a legally binding act.

AGREEMENTS WITH THIRD COUNTRIES

The CJ applies agreements with third countries as an integral part of EU law. There are three types:

1   agreements between the Union and one or more third countries;

2 'mixed' agreements between the Union and Member States and the Union and third countries;

3 agreements between Member States and third countries which are only part of EU law in exceptional circumstances.

COMPETENCE AND LEGAL BASIS

When enacting legislation, the EU institutions must ensure that:

- the proposal is adopted on the correct legal basis and in accordance with the correct legislative procedure as set out in the Treaties (see Chapter 3);

- the proposal is published and reasons are given for its enactment;

- if competence is shared between the Union and the Member States, the proposal complies with the principles of proportionality and subsidiarity.

Failure to comply with these obligations will give rise to its validity being challenged before the Court of Justice (or before the General Court if an individual brings an action) in accordance with Article 263 TFEU (formerly Article 230 TEC). A successful action renders the act void.

It is important to note that the Union can only enact new secondary legislation where it has competence to do so as conferred by the Treaties. In most cases, this is straightforward as there will be a *specific* power to legislate clearly referred to in the relevant Treaties article. In addition, there are *general* legislative powers laid down in the Treaty in Articles 114, 115 and 352 TFEU (formerly Articles 94, 95 and 308 TEC) which may be relied upon if the Treaties do not lay down a specific power.

- **Article 114 TFEU (ex Article 95 TEC)** – A broader, residual provision. It allows by way of derogation from Article 115 and 'save where otherwise provided in this Treaty' the Council to enact measures to harmonise laws 'which have as their object the establishment and functioning of the internal market' as set out in Article 26 (formerly Article 14 TEC). The co-decision procedure (Article 294 TFEU, formerly Article 251 TEC) must be followed and the Economic and Social Committee must be consulted. A number of qualifications are set out in Article 114 (2)–(10) TFEU (formerly Article 95(2)–(10) TEC).

- **Article 115 TFEU (formerly Article 94 TEC)** – Enables the Council to enact only directives which have been proposed by the Commission in order to harmonise laws which 'directly affect the establishment or functioning of the common market' by unanimity and after consulting the European Parliament and Economic and Social Committee.

- **Article 352 TFEU (formerly Article 308 TEC)** – Applicable only if a measure is required to attain one of the objectives of the EU, in the course of the operation of the common market. It requires the Council to adopt a measure proposed by the Commission by unanimity after consulting the European Parliament.

Disagreements as to the validity of a EU act have arisen between the EU institutions and/or Member States where a Treaty article is not clear or may be interpreted in a number of ways.

The *Working Time Directive case* [1996] is a clear example of a conflict arising over competence. In this case, the UK sought to have a directive regulating the organisation of working time annulled in accordance with the action for annulment set out in Art 263 TFEU (formerly Art 230 TEC). The directive had been adopted in accordance with Article 153 TFEU (formerly Art 137 TEC), which relates to health and safety by qualified majority voting in the Council. The UK argued that the directive was not a health and safety measure, but a broader social policy measure. Consequently, the directive should have been adopted in accordance with Article 115 TFEU (formerly Article 94 TEC) or Article 352 TFEU (formerly Article 308 TEC) which require unanimity in the Council. This would have meant that the UK could have vetoed the proposed directive. The CJ disagreed with the UK and held that Article 153 TFEU (formerly Article 137 TEC) was the correct legal base.

> ▶ **UNITED KINGDOM v COUNCIL (WORKING TIME DIRECTIVE CASE) [1996]**
>
> The UK challenged the enactment of the Working Time Directive on the grounds that it had been adopted on the wrong legal base and should have been adopted by unanimity rather than by qualified majority voting. This would have enabled the UK to veto the new measure.

> The Court of Justice rejected the UK's arguments and held that the directive was a health and safety measure and had been adopted on the correct legal base.

The situation is also problematic where competence is shared between the EU and the Member States. Traditionally, where there is conflict, it has been left to the Court of Justice to decide on the division of competence. The Treaty of Lisbon sets out a much clearer demarcation of the division of competence between the EU and the Member States.

PROPORTIONALITY AND SUBSIDIARITY

Article 5 TEU (formerly Art 5 TEC) seeks to ensure that the EU institutions act within the bounds of their competence as set out in the Treaty. The TEU added that where competence is shared between the EU and the Member States, the principles of proportionality and subsidiarity must be complied with. This means that the EU must show that the proposed act does not go beyond what is necessary to achieve the objective sought and that the EU is better placed to act than national or even regional authorities.

Article 5 TEU (formerly Art 5 TEC) states that:

1. The limits of Union competences are governed by the principle of conferral. The use of Union competences is governed by the principles of subsidiarity and proportionality.
2. Under the principle of *conferral*, the Union shall act only within the limits of the competences conferred upon it by the Member States in the Treaties to attain the objectives set out therein. Competences not conferred upon the Union in the Treaties remain with the Member States.
3. Under the principle of *subsidiarity*, in areas which do not fall within its exclusive competence, the Union shall act only if and in so far as the objectives of the proposed action cannot be sufficiently achieved by the Member States, either at central level or at regional and local level, but can rather, by reason of the scale or effects of the proposed action, be better achieved at Union level. (. . .)

4.   Under the principle of *proportionality*, the content and form of Union action shall not exceed what is necessary to achieve the objectives of the Treaties. (. . .)

The 1993 Inter-Institutional Agreement on Procedures for Implementing the Principle of Subsidiarity requires all three political institutions to comply with the principle when enacting legislation. This commitment was re-confirmed by the Protocol on the Application of the Principles of Subsidiarity and Proportionality which was attached to the Treaty of Amsterdam (ToA).

The Court of Justice has been called upon to review the compatibility of EU legislation with the principle of subsidiarity in a number of cases: *United Kingdom v Council (Working Time Directive case)* [1996]; *Germany v European Parliament and Council* [1997]; *Germany v European Parliament and Council (Tobacco Advertising Case)* [2000]. However, the CJ has been reluctant to judicially review compatibility with the principle of subsidiarity in any depth and has yet to declare an act invalid for failure to comply with the principle.

DECISIONS OF THE COURT OF JUSTICE (FORMERLY EUROPEAN COURT OF JUSTICE – ECJ) AND THE GENERAL COURT (FORMERLY COURT OF FIRST INSTANCE – CFI)

Case law of the Court of Justice (CJ) (formerly ECJ) and the General Court (GC) (formerly CFI) is an important source of EU law. The Treaties and secondary legislation cannot cater for all situations or social and economic developments, and much of the work of the Court of Justice and the General Court has been to fill the gaps in the law, and to interpret the Treaties and secondary legislation in accordance with the general objectives of the Treaties.

Some of the most important principles of EU law have been developed by the CJ, e.g. the principle of direct effect, the principle of indirect effect, state liability for breach of EU law, and the principle of supremacy of EU law (now confirmed by the Lisbon Treaty).

You should now be confident that you would be able to tick all of the boxes on the checklist at the beginning of this chapter. To check your knowledge of the Establishment of the EU and sources of law why not visit the companion website and take the Multiple Choice Question test. Check your understanding of the terms and vocabulary used in this chapter with the flashcard glossary.

2

Relationship between EU law and national law

Distinguish between direct applicability and direct effect ☐

Understand when a Treaties article, regulation and decision have direct effect ☐

Distinguish between vertical and horizontal direct effect ☐

Recognise when a directive has direct effect and be able to apply the criteria to a problem question ☐

Know what is meant by the principle of indirect effect and recognise its limitations ☐

Identify the criteria for the application of the Francovich principle ☐

Understand that the principle of effectiveness demands that national remedies and national procedural rules cannot make the exercise of EU law rights difficult or impossible to pursue, and that the principle of equivalence requires that EU law actions cannot be treated less favourably than comparable actions derived from domestic law ☐

Understand how the Court of Justice (formerly ECJ) has developed the principle of supremacy of EU law ☐

DIRECT EFFECT

DIRECT EFFECT OF TREATIES PROVISIONS

Usually, international Treaties are agreements between governments and do not create rights for citizens enforceable before national courts.

The EU legal order differs from international law in this respect, as it does create rights for citizens which are enforceable before national courts. This is what is meant by direct effect.

The concept started with the case of *Van Gend en Loos v Nederlandse Administratie der Belastingen* [1963]. A private firm sought to invoke EU law against Dutch customs authorities in proceedings before a Dutch tribunal. A preliminary reference was made to the Court of Justice (CJ) (previously ECJ). The Dutch Government argued that an infringement of the Treaty did not give an individual the right to bring an action. Actions could only be brought against the government of a Member State by the Commission.

It was held that the Treaty created a 'new legal order' and created rights for individuals which became part of their legal heritage.

Directly effective EU law is that which gives rise to rights or obligations which individuals may enforce before their national courts.

Van Gend en Loos was brought on the basis of Art 30 TFEU (formerly Art 25 TEC) which is a negative obligation as it requires that Member States shall refrain from introducing any new customs duties on imports and exports.

The concept was extended in the case of *Alfons Lütticke GmbH v Commission* [1966], where it was held that a positive obligation could have direct effect once the time limit for implementation has expired.

The criteria for a provision to have direct effect were set out by AG Mayras, in *Reyners v Belgium* [1974], as follows:

- the provision must be clear and unambiguous;

- it must be unconditional;

- its operation must not be dependent on further action being taken by the Community (now Union) or national authorities.

In *Defrenne v SABENA (No 2)* the court conditioned the direct effect on the provision to be sufficiently precise and unconditional. It can be deduced from this that certain provisions of the Treaty are not directly effective as they are too vague. Neither must there be any discretion attached to the implementation of the provision, nor must the right be dependent on some legislative or executive action of the Commission or a Member State, until such action has been taken or the time limit for taking action has expired.

Van Gend en Loos is an example of what is known as vertical direct effect: a party invokes a provision of EU law in a national court against a Member State. It was held in *Defrenne v SABENA (No 2)* [1976] that Treaty obligations could be imposed on individuals as well as Member States. If a party invokes a provision of EU law in a national court against a private party, this is called horizontal direct effect. The applicant was an air stewardess employed by SABENA. She brought an action against them based on Art 157 TFEU (formerly Art 141 TEC) which provides that men and women shall receive equal pay for equal work. The applicant claimed that male air stewards were paid more for performing exactly the same tasks as stewardesses and this was a breach of Art 157 TFEU. SABENA had argued that the Treaty obligations could not be imposed on private persons as well as the State. The CJ disagreed.

> ## ▶ DEFRENNE v SABENA (No 2) [1976]
>
> **An airline stewardess claiming equal pay as a male cabin steward relied on Art 157 TFEU (formerly Art 141 EC) of the EC Treaty.**
>
> **The CJ ruled that a Treaty article has both vertical and horizontal direct effect provided that it is sufficiently precise and unconditional, i.e. it gave rights which could be enforced in a national court.**

Other Treaties Articles capable of imposing obligations on individuals are Art 45 TFEU (formerly Art 39 EC), which provides for the free movement of workers (*Angonese* [2000]), and Arts 101 and 102 TFEU (formerly Arts 81 and 82 TEC), which deal with competition law (*Courage Ltd v Crehan* [2001]).

DIRECT APPLICABILITY

In addition to direct effect, there is a principle of 'direct applicability', which means that a provision becomes operative in a Member State immediately, without the need for the national legislature to pass implementing legislation to incorporate it into national law.

The terms 'direct applicability' and 'direct effect' have been used interchangeably by the ECJ, yet they are separate concepts. A provision can be directly applicable in the sense that it forms part of the law of a Member State in the absence of implementing legislation and yet not be sufficiently precise to have direct effect.

Conversely, an EU provision can be sufficiently precise to be relied on before a national court even though it has not been transposed into national law.

DIRECT APPLICABILITY OF REGULATIONS

Article 288 TFEU (formerly Art 249 TEC) states that 'a regulation shall have general application. It shall be binding in its entirety and directly applicable in all Member States'.

As regulations are directly applicable in the same way as Treaty provisions, they do not need national implementing legislation. The CJ went further in *Leonesio* [1972], where it said that not only is national implementing legislation unnecessary, it is illegal.

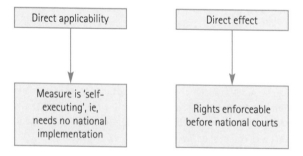

The CJ felt that there would be three main dangers if regulations were to be implemented into national law:

1   it would be unclear whether they took effect from the date of the national measure or the date of the Community measure;

2   there would be subtle changes made to a regulation when transferred to national legislation;

3   it could prejudice the CJ's jurisdiction to give a ruling on the interpretation and validity of the measure for the procedure for a preliminary reference.

Nevertheless, there are exceptions to the rule that regulations do not need national implementing legislation:

■ where the regulation expressly requires national implementing legislation: *Commission v United Kingdom* (*Tachograph* case) [1979];

■ where a regulation impliedly requires that a Member State brings forward national legislation, for example, where the terms of a regulation are vague, though the national legislation must not be incompatible with the regulation.

DIRECT EFFECT OF DIRECTIVES

Article 288 TFEU (formerly Art 249 TEC) states that directives are 'binding as to the result to be achieved' but that the choice of 'form and methods' is left to the Member State.

In contrast to regulations, the Treaty does not make any reference to directives being directly applicable. They cannot be directly applicable as they require national implementing legislation to give effect to them.

Despite the Treaty being silent on the point, the CJ found that directives could have direct effect in *Van Duyn v Home Office* [1974].

▶ VAN DUYN v HOME OFFICE [1974]

The CJ held that Directive 64/221 (which provided that measures taken on grounds of public policy or public security shall be based exclusively on the personal conduct of the individual) was sufficiently precise to have direct effect.

The main reasons why the CJ gave direct effect to directives were:

■ to make them more effective;

■ to estop a Member State from relying on its own wrongdoing: *Ratti* [1979].

There was a strong reaction against giving direct effect to directives in the Member States, and the French Conseil d'État and initially the German Federal Tax Court denied that directives had direct effect.

The CJ took this reaction into account, and in addition to having to satisfy the criteria for direct effect, the CJ has placed two other important limitations on the direct effect of directives:

1   they cannot have direct effect before the time limit for implementation has expired: *Ratti* [1979];
2   they do not have horizontal direct effect: *Marshall v Southampton and South West Hampshire AHA (No 1)* [1986].

▶ RATTI [1979]

In his defence against a prosecution brought by the Italian state, Mr. Ratti sought to rely on an unimplemented directive.

The CJ ruled that a directive has direct effect if it is clear and unconditional, the time for implementation has passed and the other party to the proceedings is the state.

A directive can be directly effective, and may be invoked as such, even though it has been transposed into national law: *VNO v Inspecteur der Invoerrechten en Accijnzen* [1977]; *Marks and Spencer* [2002].

The disadvantages of giving only vertical direct effect to directives have been identified as follows:

■ the effectiveness of directives within the national legal system is restricted;

■ the uniform application of EU law is restricted;

■ there is discrimination between individuals. For example, in employment law, a State employee can rely on a directive as against an employer, whereas a private employee cannot.

As a result of these difficulties, the CJ has had to develop various strategies to circumvent the problems created by this limitation of the direct effect of directives (see below):

- broad interpretation of the 'State';

- interpretative obligation (principle of indirect effect);

- 'incidental horizontal direct effect';

- *Francovich* principle (principle of State liability).

The CJ was asked to reconsider its position in the cases of *Faccini Dori* [1994] and *Pfeiffer* [2004]. The ECJ refused to recognise that directives can have horizontal direct effect and reconfirmed its *Marshall (No 1)* [1986] decision. However, the CJ emphasised that individuals have other options for enforcing their Community rights, such as the principle of indirect effect and the principle of State liability (see below).

In *Arcor AG & Co KG v Bundesrepublik Deutschland* [2008] the CJ recalled that, according to settled case law, a directive cannot of itself impose obligations on an individual, but can only confer rights. Consequently, and individual may not rely on a directive [. . .] where it is a matter of State obligation directly linked to the performance of another obligation falling, pursuant to that directive, on a third party.

Organ of the State/Emanation of the State

In *Marshall (No 1)*, the UK argued that where the State was acting as an employer, its position was no different from that of a private employer. The CJ rejected this argument and held that it did not matter what capacity the State was acting in; directives could still be relied upon against it.

▶ MARSHALL (NO 1) [1986]

The applicant sought to rely on the Equal Treatment directive against her employer. As her employer was a Health Authority, and thus an organ of the state, she could rely on the directive.

In *Foster v British Gas plc* [1990], the CJ defined an 'organ of the State' as one that was offering a public service under the control of a public authority and which enjoyed special powers. The House of Lords, applying this test, held that British Gas (prior to privatisation) was an 'organ of the State'. There was some doubt as to whether the three criteria in *Foster* were alternatives or cumulative. It appears from *Rieser Internationale Transporte* [2004] that the criteria are cumulative, i.e. that a body is an emanation of the state if it provides a public service under state supervision and has for that purpose special powers.

> ### ▶ FOSTER v BRITISH GAS PLC [1990]
>
> **Mrs Foster sought to rely on the Equal Treatment directive in order to remain in work after the age of 60. The question arose as to whether British Gas was a state entity.**
>
> **The CJ ruled that a state entity provides a public service under the control of the state and has special powers.**

In *Johnston v Chief Constable of the Royal Ulster Constabulary* [1986], it was held that a directive could be relied on against a chief constable, as he is responsible for the direction of the police service. Since a police authority is charged by the State with the maintenance of public order and safety, it does not act as a private individual. On that basis, it could be regarded as an 'organ of the State'.

In *Jiménez Melgar* [2001], the claimant sought to rely upon Directive 92/85 against the Municipality of Los Barrios in southern Spain. The CJ stated that 'It is settled case-law that the Member States' obligation arising from a directive to achieve the result prescribed by the directive ... is binding on all the authorities of the Member States, including decentralised authorities such as municipalities'.

In *Doughty v Rolls-Royce plc* [1992], the English Court of Appeal held that Rolls Royce (a nationalised body at the time which was the engine manufacturer for the Royal Air Force) was not an emanation of the state. Although the company was under the control of the state, the 'public service' was provided to the state, not to the public, nor did the company enjoy special powers of the type enjoyed by British Gas in *Foster*.

In *Griffin v South-West Water Services Ltd* [1995], the English High Court held when applying the three *Foster* criteria, that South-West Water was an emanation of the state, despite being privatised. The judge made it clear that the question was not whether the body in question was under the control of the state, but whether the public service in question was under the control of the state.

DIRECT EFFECT OF DECISIONS

Under Art 288 TFEU (formerly Art 249 TEC), a decision of the Council or Commission is binding on those to whom it is addressed. It can be addressed to Member States, individuals or corporations.

Decisions were held to be directly effective in *Grad v Finanzamt Traunstein* [1970]. Again, before they can be directly effective, they must fulfil the criteria for direct effectiveness.

DIRECT EFFECT OF INTERNATIONAL AGREEMENTS

The CJ has recognised that in some circumstances international agreements can produce direct effects: *Kupferberg* [1982], *Amministrazione delle Finanze dello Stato v Chiquita Italia* [1995]. However, the ECJ has refused to recognise the direct effect of the *General Agreement on Trade and Tariffs (GATT) 1947* and *World Trade Organisation (WTO)* agreements: *International Fruit Company v Produktschap voor Groenten en Fruit* [1972], *Portugal v Council* [1999].

INTERPRETIVE OBLIGATION (INDIRECT EFFECT)

The main limitations on the direct effect of directives are that they cannot have horizontal direct effect, nor can they have direct effect before the time limit for implementation has expired. These limitations have meant that the effectiveness of directives has been seriously undermined. The CJ has created an interpretive obligation on the national courts when interpreting national legislation, which to some extent circumvents these restrictions indirectly.

The origins of the obligation lie in the case of *Von Colson and Kamman v Land Nordrhein-Westfalen* [1984]. A German prison refused to engage two female social workers who were better qualified than the men who were employed in their place.

The equal treatment principle contained in Directive 76/207 had been infringed, but the German legislation implementing the directive limited the right to compensation to a nominal sum. The directive had not specified the form of the sanction for infringement of the equal treatment principle, but it was intended to be an adequate remedy. As there was a discretion in the hands of the Member States as to how the sanction was to be implemented, the provision did not fulfil the criteria for direct effect. On a preliminary reference, the CJ used Art 4 TEU (formerly Art 10 TEC) which places Member States under an obligation to fulfil their Treaty obligations.

The CJ said that Art 4 TEU (formerly Art 10 TEC) was an obligation addressed to all national authorities, including national courts. National courts are, therefore, under an obligation to interpret national legislation in accordance with the aims and purposes of directives.

A limitation was placed on the obligation by the CJ, as it said that it only existed 'so far as it was possible' for the national court to give the national legislation a Community (now Union) interpretation. Another uncertainty created by the case was that it involved legislation which had been introduced to implement the directive, and it was unclear whether the obligation extended to legislation which was not framed with the intention of implementing a directive.

> ▶ VON COLSON [1984]
>
> **Germany had wrongly implemented a directive on equal employment rights.**
>
> The CJ ruled that Member States, including national courts, should take all appropriate measures to give effect to Community law under Art 4 TEU (formerly Art 10 TEC). Thus, national courts were required to interpret their national law in the light of the aims of the wrongly implemented directive.

The interpretive obligation was extended in the case of *Marleasing SA v La Commercial Internacional de Alimentacion SA* [1992] to all national legislation. The claimant, Marleasing, sought to set aside the memorandum and articles of association of La Commercial on the grounds that, in the view of the claimant, it had been set up to put certain assets beyond the reach of creditors. The First Company Directive 68/55 exhaustively sets out the grounds on which a company can be declared void, and does not list fraud. However, the directive had not been transposed into Spanish law. The Spanish Civil Code was enacted before the directive and so could not possibly have been brought forward with the intention of implementing the legislation. Nevertheless, the CJ said that the obligation extended to the Civil Code even though it had been enacted prior to the directive.

> ### ▶ MARLEASING [1992]
>
> **A directive which had not been implemented in Spain conflicted with the Spanish Civil Code.**
>
> The CJ ruled that pre-dated or post-dated national legislation should be interpreted in the light of the aims of an unimplemented directive.

The CJ confirmed in *Adeneler* [2006] that the interpretative duty only arises for national courts once the date for transposition of the directive has expired. However, prior to this deadline, public law bodies should avoid introducing measures which could conflict with the objective of a Directive: *Inter-Environnement Wallonie ASBL* [1997].

The CJ has introduced limitations on the national courts' interpretative duty:

- national courts are not required to interpret national law to comply with a non-transposed or incorrectly transposed directive where this would contravene the principles of legal certainty and non-retroactivity and, in particular, impose a criminal sanction upon an individual which did not otherwise exist under national law: *Kolpinghuis* [1987], *Procura della Repubblica v X* [1996], *Arcaro* [1996].

- national courts are not required to interpret national law *contra legem* ('against the law') *Wagner Miret* [1993]. The obligation only exists where it is genuinely possible to interpret national law to comply with EU law.

Nevertheless, the duty of interpretation is a strong one. In *Adeneler* [2006], the CJ held that, 'the principle that national law must be interpreted in conformity with Union law requires national courts to do whatever lies within their jurisdiction, taking the whole body of domestic law into consideration and applying interpretative methods recognised by domestic law, with a view to ensuring that the directive in question is fully effective and achieving an outcome consistent with the objective pursued by it'.

The ECJ has consistently held that if a consistent interpretation is not possible, an alternative remedy may be available under the principle of State liability (see below).

INTERPRETATIVE OBLIGATION (INDIRECT EFFECT) AND THE FORMER THIRD PILLAR (Pre-Lisbon)

Prior to the abolition of the pillar structure with the Lisbon Treaty the question arose whether Member States were obliged to interpret national law in conformity with EU framework decisions concerning third pillar issues. In *Pupino* [2005], the CJ extended the interpretative duty to framework decisions adopted under its inter-governmental third pillar. It was alleged that Italian law did not comply with provisions of Framework Decision 2001/220/JHA relating to the standing of victims in criminal proceedings adopted under the third pillar. The Italian court referred to the Court of Justice for a preliminary ruling under pre-Lisbon Article 35 TEU, a similar provision to Art 267 TFEU (formerly Article 234 TEC) under the former first pillar. Pre-Lisbon Article 34(2)(b) TEU expressly stated that Framework Decisions cannot have direct effect.

Nevertheless, the CJ noted that the pre-Lisbon Article 34(2)(b) TEU is similar in content to Article 288(3) TFEU (formerly Article 249(3) TEC) and as a result, places on national courts, an obligation to interpret national law in conformity with the Framework Decision.

> ### ▶ PUPINO [2005]
>
> **Italian criminal law did not comply with a third pillar Framework Decision designed to protect victims during criminal proceedings. Pre-Lisbon Article 34(2)(b) TEU expressly states that Framework Decisions do not have direct effect.**
>
> **The CJ held that the national court was under a duty to interpret national law to comply with the Framework Decision.**

With the entering into force of the Lisbon Treaty the pillar structure of the EU was abolished. This means that the remaining part of the justice and home affairs, namely the police and judicial co-operation in criminal matters, has moved from the sphere of intergovernmental co-operation into the realm of the EU method. Framework decisions no longer exist and can be replaced by full catalogue of institutional acts of European Union – regulations, directives and decisions. The third pillar will be subject to the general EU principles. Nevertheless, the ruling in *Pupino* provides an alternative basis for indirect effect which is the general obigation residing in the objective of ever closer union set out in Art 1(2) TEU.

INCIDENTAL HORIZONTAL DIRECT EFFECT

Following the ECJ's decision in *CIA Security International SA v Signalson SA and Securitel SPRL* [1996], there was some uncertainty as to whether the CJ had changed its view on whether a private party can rely on a directive in proceedings against another private party, as laid down in *Faccini Dori* [1994].

In *CIA*, the claimant had brought proceedings against the two defendants in the Belgian courts, alleging unfair trading practices. The defendants claimed that the alarm system which was marketed by the claimant had not been approved as required by Belgian law. The claimant alleged that it was libelled by the defendants' claims and argued that it had not sought approval because the Belgian legislation breached EU law and, in particular, Article 8 of Directive 83/189, which requires that the Member State notify the Commission about the technical standards of the alarms. On a referral to the CJ, the Court held that the Belgian law had breached EC law and was, therefore, inapplicable to individuals. The CJ's ruling meant that CIA, a private company, could rely on the directive as a defence to the claim made by defendants.

The situation in the *CIA* case has become known as the concept of 'incidental horizontal direct effect' and it will only arise in limited, exceptional circumstances.

In *Lemmens* [1998], the claimant tried to argue that the failure to notify the Commission about a breathalyser machine meant that the results of a breathalyser test could not be used against him in drink-driving proceedings. The CJ rejected this argument and held that the *CIA* rule only applies to legislation which affects trade between Member States and did not apply in this case.

However, the ECJ controversially re-affirmed and extended the *CIA* principle in *Unilever Italia* [2000]. A draft Italian law on olive oil had been notified to the Commission under Article 8 of Directive 83/189. The Commission informed the Italian authorities that it intended to legislate in this area, thereby triggering the additional nine month standstill provision under Article 9. Italy nevertheless went ahead and adopted legislation in August 1998. In September 1998, on receipt of an order from Central Food, Unilever supplied 648 litres of olive oil. The next day, Central Food informed Unilever that it would not pay for the olive oil as it had not been labelled in accordance with the contested Italian law. Unilever argued that since the national law had been adopted in breach of the standstill clause in Article 9, the principle of non-enforceability laid down in the *CIA* case in respect of Article 8 also applied to Article 9 and so it was not obliged to comply with the Italian law and Central Food should pay what it owed.

Advocate-General Jacobs disagreed with Unilever since traders should not be considered to be experts in EU law and are unlikely to know if a Member State has complied with the directive in question. However, the ECJ followed its ruling in *CIA*. It held that failure to postpone the adoption of the new law in accordance with the directive rendered the national legislation inapplicable.

In view of the uncertainty that had arisen, the CJ took the opportunity in *Unilever* to address the issue of horizontal direct effect of directives. It re-affirmed that directives cannot have horizontal direct effect but it also recognised an exception to this rule in cases involving substantial procedural defects. The ECJ distinguished between two different kinds of directives:

- Where a directive regulates relations between individuals and aims to approximate laws by conferring rights and obligations on individuals, e.g. Package Holidays Directive, the orthodox rule applies (no horizontal direct effect of directives).

- Where a directive involves institutional relations like Directive 83/189 and its aim is to protect the principle of free movement of goods by means of a preventive control mechanism such as notifications, it creates neither rights nor obligations for individuals. The orthodox rule of 'no horizontal direct effect of directives' does not apply.

Although the CJ's decisions in *CIA* and *Unilever* have led to a huge increase in the number of notifications (and withdrawals) of national technical rules by the Member States, which has increased the effective enforcement of the free movement of goods, the law creates legal uncertainty. Commercial organisations may not know that a national law that they have complied with in good faith is not applicable.

> ▶ UNILEVER [2000]
>
> Italy adopted a new law regulating the olive oil market contrary to Directive 83/189 which requires Member States to notify the Commission of any new technical rules it wishes to introduce and await a response. Unilever sold olive oil to Central Foods which did not comply with the Italian law. Central Foods refused to pay. Unilever argued that the law had been introduced in breach of the Directive and sought to rely on the Directive in its dispute with another private party.
>
> The CJ held that the Italian law had been introduced in breach of the Directive and could not apply.

STATE LIABILITY IN DAMAGES

LIABILITY FOR NON-IMPLEMENTATION OF A DIRECTIVE

In *Francovich and Bonifaci v Italy* [1991], the applicants had been employees in businesses which became insolvent, leaving substantial arrears of salary unpaid. The Italian government had failed to implement a directive that would oblige them to set up a compensation scheme to protect employees of insolvent employers. This breach had been proved in enforcement proceedings taken against Italy by the Commission.

The provisions of the directive did not have direct effect. Nevertheless, the CJ held that Art 4 TEU (formerly Art 10 TEC) requires Member States to fulfil their EC obligations, that the effectiveness of EU law would be called into question and the protection of EC law rights would be weakened, if individuals could not obtain compensation when their rights were infringed. On this basis, it was said to be inherent in the scheme of the Treaties that individuals should receive compensation from a Member State when it had breached its EU obligations. This right is subject to three conditions:

1   the directive must confer rights on individuals;
2   the content of these rights must be identifiable by reference to the directive;
3   there must be a causal link between the breach of a State's obligation and the damage suffered by the persons affected.

> ### ▶ FRANCOVICH [1991]

> **In breach of EU law, Italy failed to set up a scheme to compensate workers on the insolvency of their employers and a claim was brought by Mr Francovich.**

> **The CJ ruled that Italy was in breach of its obligations and was liable in principle to compensate Mr Francovich who had suffered loss as a result of that breach.**

LIABILITY FOR BREACHES OTHER THAN NON-IMPLEMENTATION OF A DIRECTIVE

The decision in *Francovich* left open a number of questions, including whether the State was under a liability to compensate for breaches of a directly effective Treaty provision or whether the State was liable where it had implemented a directive but the implementation was subsequently discovered to be incorrect.

The joined cases of *Factortame (No 3)* and *Brasserie du Pêcheur* [1996] dealt with the question of State liability for breaches of a directly effective Treaty provision. In the first case, the applicants, a group of Spanish fishermen, claimed damages as a result of not being able to fish in British waters during the period of 1 April 1989 to 2 November 1989 when the Merchant Shipping Act 1988 had laid down certain restrictions relating to the nationality, domicile and residence of the owners and managers of fishing vessels and of share-holders and directors of vessel owning and managing companies. These restrictions were designed to discourage 'quota hopping' in the fishing industry and had been found to be in breach of Art 49 TFEU (formerly Art 43 TEC) in earlier enforcement proceedings. In *Brasserie du Pêcheur*, the claimant had been prevented from exporting French beer to Germany as a result of German beer purity laws. These laws prevented the use of certain ingredients in the brewing of beer and prohibited the use of additives in beer altogether. The German law had been held to be in breach of Art 34 TFEU (formerly Art 28 TEC) in earlier enforcement proceedings brought in 1987. The French brewers sued the German Government for compensation for the period that they had been unable to export beer to Germany.

The CJ held that there could be liability for State breaches of directly effective Treaties provisions. This principle of State liability includes acts of the legislature which are in breach of Union law and is inherent in the scheme of the Treaty. The Court noted that in both cases the legislature had a wide discretion. In *Factortame*, its discretion concerned the registration of fishing vessels, whereas in *Brasserie du Pêcheur* its discretion covered the regulation of foodstuffs.

The discretion enjoyed by these legislatures was analogous to that of Community institutions when enacting Union legislation. In these circumstances, there would be liability where three conditions were satisfied:

1   the rule of law must be intended to confer rights on individuals;
2   the breach must be sufficiently serious;
3   there must be a direct causal link between the breach of the obligation and the damage suffered by the parties.

It is for a national court to determine whether these criteria have been satisfied. These principles have been developed by reference to Art 340 TFEU (formerly Art 288 of the EC Treaty), which is the provision dealing with the liability of EU institutions. What is striking is that the fact that a Member State has breached EU law is not, in itself, sufficient to ensure compensation. The breach must be 'sufficiently serious'.

The CJ provided some guidance as to what would constitute a sufficiently serious breach. The decisive test was whether the Member State had 'manifestly and gravely disregarded the limits on its discretion'. The factors which could be taken into account by a national court were:

▪   the clarity and precision of the rule breached;

▪   the measure of discretion left to national or EU authorities;

▪   whether the infringement and damage caused was intentional or voluntary;

▪   whether any error of law was excusable;

- the fact that a position taken by a EU institution might have contributed to the omission;

- the adoption or retention of measures contrary to EU law.

Any breach which persisted after a judgment in enforcement proceedings or where there had been a preliminary ruling or settled case law of the Court, so that it was clear that the conduct in question constituted an infringement, would be 'sufficiently serious'. The CJ made it clear that discrimination on grounds of nationality, as in *Factortame (No 3)*, would be sufficiently serious.

▶ FACTORTAME (NO 3) [1996]

This case involved the Merchant Shipping Act 1988, **which was in breach of Art 49 TFEU (formerly Art 43 TEC) which provides for the right of establishment.**

In this case (joined with *Brasserie du Pêcheur* **above), the CJ redefined the conditions for state liability for breach of EC law.**

See also *Brasserie du Pêcheur SA v Germany* **below.**

When *Brasserie du Pêcheur* returned to the German Federal Court, it had found that the incompatibility of the German beer purity laws with Art 34 TFEU (formerly Art 28 TEC) was not conclusive before the Commission had successfully taken enforcement proceedings against Germany. In the opinion of the German court, the case law of the CJ on the question of the use of additives was not conclusive before 1987. The German court went on to decide that the cause of the beer's ban from the German market was the use of additives. Consequently, there was no direct causal link between the breach of Art 34 TFEU (formerly Art 28 TEC) by the German rule and the loss suffered by the claimants. They failed to receive any compensation.

▶ BRASSERIE DU PÊCHEUR [1996]

The case concerned a German beer purity law which breached Art 34 TFEU (formerly Art 28 TEC).

The CJ ruled that a state incurs liability for breach of EU law if the rule of EU law confers rights on individuals, the breach is

sufficiently serious and there is a causal link between the breach and the individual's loss.

See also *R v Secretary of State for Transport ex parte Factortame Ltd* above.

When the House of Lords gave judgment in *R v Secretary of State for Transport ex p Factortame (No 5)* [1999], it held that the British legislation was discriminatory on grounds of nationality, in breach of clear and unambiguous rules of EU law, and was sufficiently serious to give rise to a right to damages for individuals who had suffered loss. As a result, the UK Government faced a £30 million bill for compensation.

The case of *R v Minister of Agriculture, Fisheries and Food ex p Hedley Lomas* [1996] concerned the refusal of the UK Government to issue licences for the export of live animals to Spain as it felt that standards in slaughter houses there contravened a directive. Hedley Lomas, a company, had been refused an export licence and claimed that it was a breach of Art 35 TFEU (formerly Art 29 TEC). The CJ stated that the mere infringement of Union law might be 'sufficiently serious' where the Member State was not called upon to make any legislative choices and had reduced or no discretion. The UK had not even proved that the Spanish slaughter houses were falling below the standards laid down in the directive.

The question of an incorrect transposition of a directive was considered in *R v HM Treasury ex p British Telecommunications plc* [1996]. The CJ held that the provision of the directive in question was imprecise and was reasonably capable of bearing the meaning ascribed to it by the UK Government. The interpretation had been shared by other Member States and was not contrary to the wording or objective of the directive. Despite having said previously that it is a matter for a national court to determine whether the criteria for liability have been satisfied, it said in this case that it was in possession of all the information and that the breach was not 'sufficiently serious'. Although the UK was in breach of Union law, this did not give the company affected a right to compensation, as the breach was not 'sufficiently serious'.

The test for State liability in the event of a non-implementation of a directive was clarified by the CJ in *Dillenkofer* [1996]. The German government failed to implement a directive concerned with the protection of individuals who bought package holidays. As a result of this failure, the applicants had suffered financial loss when their travel companies became insolvent. The CJ held that the criteria laid down in *Factortame (No. 3)* and *Brasserie du Pêcheur* would apply. It held that where a provision has direct effect, the first condition is automatically satisfied. It also stated that where a Member State fails to implement a directive by the prescribed date, this in itself amounts to a sufficiently serious breach of Union law and satisfies the second limb of the test.

Other state liability claims based on incorrectly implemented directives include *Rechberger & Others v Austria* [1999] and *Stockholm Lindöpark v Sweden* [2001]. In both cases the claimants were successful. In *Rechberger* the claimants argued that Austria had imposed limitations on consumers' rights when implementing Art 7 of Directive 90/314. The CJ agreed that there was no 'margin of discretion' as to the wording of the implementing legislation, the Austrian legislation was, therefore, 'manifestly incompatible' with the obligations under the directive and thus a sufficiently serious breach of Union law had occurred. In *Stockholm Lindöpark* the question was whether Sweden had correctly implemented the sixth VAT directive.

The Court held not, stating: 'Given the clear wording of the Sixth Directive, the Member State concerned was not in a position to make any legislative choices . . .'.

In *Haim v Kassenzahnärztliche Vereinigung Nordrhein* [2000] it was held that compensation for non-compliance with Union law could be claimed with regard to the actions of a public body, as well as those of a Member State. Furthermore, it was held that the compensation could be claimed directly from the public body. The result is that a public body may be held financially accountable for non-compliance even if its actions were limited by national legislation.

Köbler

In *Köbler v Austria* [2003], the CJ held that there was no reason why a *Francovich* claim could not be brought against a national court of last resort. K, an Austrian national, had brought an unsuccessful challenge to a provision of Austrian legislation, which he alleged contravened his rights under Art 45 TFEU (formerly Art 39 TEC) (see Chapter 5). However, the Austrian Supreme Court rejected his claim. K then brought a *Francovich* action, asserting that the Austrian court had misapplied an earlier CJ ruling, that this constituted a 'sufficiently serious breach' and that he was, therefore, entitled to compensation. The CJ agreed that, in principle, K's claim was valid. The same conditions applied as in any *Francovich* claim, although it was said that 'liability can be incurred only in the exceptional case where the national court has manifestly infringed the applicable law and the Court's case-law in the matter'. Applying this point, the CJ decided that, although the Austrian court had committed a breach of Union law, it was not sufficiently serious.

> ### ▶ KÖBLER
>
> Mr Köbler brought an action for damages against the Austrian State for failure by the Austrian Supreme Court to apply Community law correctly. He did not succeed because the breach of Union law by the Austrian court was not sufficiently serious.

NATIONAL PROCEDURAL RULES AND REMEDIES

There is very little harmonising legislation which specifies which courts, procedures or remedies should be followed when pursuing an action for breach of EU law. Initially, national procedural rules and remedies applied. However, the CJ has gradually introduced minimum EU standards with which national law must comply in order to provide effective protection for individuals whose EU rights have been breached. In some circumstances, the CJ has gone so far as to introduce new EU remedies. The principle of State liability laid down in *Francovich* is an example of this latter approach (see above).

The CJ's first intrusion into what is called 'national procedural autonomy' was in the cases of *Rewe-Zentralfinanz eG v Landwirtschaftskammer für das Saarland* [1976] and *Comet* [1976]. The CJ held that by virtue of Art 4 TEU (formerly Art 10 TEC), national courts are under a duty to protect directly effective EU law rights. In the absence of EU harmonisation, the national laws designating the courts having jurisdiction and the procedures which must be followed should be applied subject to the following two provisos:

▓ The national rules are not less favourable than those relating to similar actions of a domestic nature (known as the principle of equivalence or non-discrimination).

RELATIONSHIP BETWEEN EU LAW AND NATIONAL LAW

■ The national rules do not make it 'impossible in practice to exercise rights which the national courts have a duty to protect' (known as the principle of effectiveness).

▶ REWE-ZENTRALFINANZ EG v LANDWIRTSCHAFTSKAMMER FÜR DAS SAARLAND and COMET [1976]

In both cases, two companies had been charged duties on products in breach of the TFEU (formerly EC Treaty). They subsequently brought actions against the national authorities for the sums illegally levied, but their claims failed because the national time-limits had expired.

The CJ held that national procedural rules apply to claims based on Union law (including national time limits), as long as they are not less favourable than those which apply to similar claims based on national law and do not make it virtually impossible in practice to bring a claim (which was not the case here even though the time limits were relatively short).

In the 1980s, the CJ's case law was bolder as it started to prioritise 'effective judicial protection' of individuals' Community rights over respect for national procedural autonomy. In several cases, the CJ introduced uniform Community standards of protection:

■ Community right to reclaim sums illegally levied: *Pigs and Bacon Commission v McCarren* [1979];

■ Community right to effective and adequate compensation: *Von Colson* [1983];

■ Community right to full compensation including interest: *Marshall (No. 2)* [1993];

■ Community right of access to effective judicial control: *Johnston* [1986];

■ Union right to a statement of reasons: *Heylens* [1987];

■ Union right to interim relief: *Factortame (No. 1)* [1990]; *Zuckerfabrik Süderdithmarschen AG v Hauptzollamt Itzehoe* [1991]; *Atlanta v BEF* [1996];

■ Union right to damages for breach of Union law: *Francovich* [1991].

Several commentators have argued that since its *Francovich* decision in 1991, the Court has been trying to address the tension in its case law between respecting national procedural autonomy and ensuring the effective protection of an individuals' Union rights and has sought to grant more discretion to national courts rather than impose Union standards: Tridimas (2001) 38 C.M.L.Rev. 301; Arnull, *The European Union and its Court of Justice*, Oxford: OUP (1999). Nevertheless, in some cases, the CJ has continued to introduce new Union standards. In its *Courage* judgment [2001], the CJ introduced a new remedy of 'individual liability' and held that private parties can bring an action for damages against other private parties for breach of the EU competition law rules laid down in Articles 101 and 102 TFEU (formerly Articles 81 and 82 TEC): *Drake* (2006) *European Law Review*, 841.

PRIMACY OF EU LAW

TWIN PILLARS

The EU legal order is said to be built on the 'twin pillars' of direct effect and supremacy. The EU Treaty in the consolidated version as amended by the Lisbon Treaty, for the first time contains an express provision regarding the supremacy of EU law.

It is the CJ which has developed the principle of supremacy along with the first pillar of direct effect.

The case of *Van Gend en Loos* [1963] is better known for introducing the other pillar of the legal order, namely, the principle of direct effect. However, it is implicit in the CJ's ruling that EU law takes precedence over national law in the event of a conflict.

> ❯ VAN GEND EN LOOS [1963]
>
> The CJ ruled that Art 30 TFEU (formerly Art 25 TEC) requiring Member States to refrain from introducing new customs duties, was unconditional and gave rise to rights and obligations which could be enforced in national courts.

The second pillar of the supremacy of EU law was expressly set out for the first time in the case of *Costa v ENEL* [1964]. The CJ held that Union law could not be overridden by domestic legal provisions, regardless of whether the provisions came earlier or later than Union law.

The 'twin pillars' of the European legal order

The basis of the principle of supremacy was found to arise from the words and spirit of the Treaty rather than in national constitutions. This can be seen from a famous *dictum* of the ECJ in *Costa v ENEL*:

> ❱ **COSTA v ENEL [1964]**
>
> The transfer by the States from their domestic legal system to the EU legal system of rights and obligations arising under the Treaties carries with it the permanent limitation of their sovereign rights against which a subsequent unilateral act incompatible with the concept of the EU cannot prevail.

The court argued that a restriction of sovereign rights and the creation of a body of law applicable to individuals, as well as Member States, made it necessary for this new legal order to override inconsistent provisions of national law.

EU law overrules provisions of national constitutions
This rule is an unconditional rule and applies to every rule of domestic law, whatever its standing. Consequently, EU law cannot be tested in municipal courts for compliance with constitutions of Member States.

In *Internationale Handelsgesellschaft mbH v Einfuhr und Vorratsstelle für Getreide* [1970], it was held that recourse to the legal rules or concepts of national law in order to judge the validity of measures adopted by the

Community would have an adverse effect on the uniformity and efficacy of Union law.

Therefore, the validity of an EU measure or its effect within a Member State cannot be affected by allegations that it runs counter to either fundamental rights, as formulated by the constitution of that State, or the principles of a national constitutional structure.

Principle of supremacy must be applied immediately

Supremacy is a rule which is addressed to the national courts and is to be applied immediately by every national court.

In *Amministrazione delle Finanze dello Stato v Simmenthal SpA* [1978], an Italian court was faced with a conflict between a Council regulation and Italian laws, some of which were subsequent in time to the Italian regulation. Under Italian law, legislation contrary to EU regulations can be declared unconstitutional, but only by the constitutional court and not by ordinary courts. The Italian judge made a preliminary reference on the question of whether direct applicability of regulations required national courts to disregard inconsistent subsequent national legislation without waiting for relevant legislation to be enacted by the national legislature.

It was held that every national court must apply Union law in its entirety and must accordingly set aside any provision of national law which may conflict with it.

If national law impairs the effectiveness of EU law by withholding the power to set aside an inconsistent piece of national law, then that rule is contrary to EU law.

Member States cannot plead *force majeure*

A Member State cannot say that it has tried to comply with an obligation or remedy a breach but has been prevented by legislation from doing so.

In *Commission v Italy* (*First Art Treasures* case) [1968], an Italian tax on art treasures was in violation of Italy's obligation under Art 30 TFEU to abolish customs duties on exports. The CJ held that, by continuing to levy the tax, Italy was in breach of Union law. Legislation had been introduced but lapsed with the dissolution of the Italian Parliament. The Government's inability to force the legislation through was not an excuse for failing to give effect to the principle of supremacy.

Supremacy applies regardless of source of law

The principle applies regardless of the *source* of national law. Both inconsistent statutes and judicial precedents have been declared inapplicable, and rules of professional bodies may also be held inconsistent and inapplicable: *R v Royal Pharmaceutical Society of Great Britain* [1989].

Supremacy applies regardless of form of EU law

The principle of supremacy applies to different forms of EU law. Consequently, it will apply whether the EU provision is a Treaty Article, an EU act or an agreement with a third country.

Member States must repeal conflicting legislation

Member States are obliged to repeal conflicting national legislation, even though it is merely 'inapplicable' and not enforced: *Commission v France* (*French Merchant Seamen* case) [1974].

A French law provided that a certain proportion of the crew on French merchant ships had to be of French nationality. This was in conflict with Union law, and enforcement proceedings were brought against France. The French Government argued that the law had not been applied and, as it was regarded as inapplicable, France had not violated the Treaties.

The CJ held that the existence of the law created 'an ambiguous state of affairs', which would make seamen uncertain as to the possibilities available to them of relying on Union law. It was not enough simply not to enforce the law: it had to be repealed.

You should now be confident that you would be able to tick all of the boxes on the checklist at the beginning of this chapter. To check your knowledge of Relationship between EU law and national law why not visit the companion website and take the Multiple Choice Question test. Check your understanding of the terms and vocabulary used in this chapter with the flashcard glossary.

3

European Union institutions

Explain the composition and functions of the three political
institutions, i.e. the Commission, the Council and the European
Parliament ☐

Understand the supervisory role of the European Parliament over
the Commission and, to a lesser extent, the Council ☐

Criticise the current institutional structure ☐

Understand the role of the European Council ☐

Describe in outline the decision making process ☐

Explain the composition of the Court of Justice (CJ) (formerly
ECJ) and General Court (GC) (formerly CFI) and their jurisdiction ☐

Discuss the procedure in the Court of Justice (CJ) (formerly ECJ) ☐

THE INSTITUTIONAL FRAMEWORK

Article 13(1) TEU reads:

> 'The Union shall have an institutional framework which shall aim to promote its values, advance its objectives, serve its interests, those of its citizens and those of the Member States, and ensure the consistency, effectiveness and continuity of its policies and actions.

The Union's institutions shall be:

- the European Parliament,
- the European Council,
- the Council,
- the European Commission (hereinafter referred to as "the Commission");
- the Court of Justice of the European Union,
- the European Central Bank,
- the Court of Auditors.'

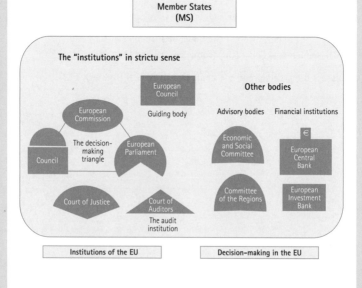

THE COMMISSION

FUNCTIONS

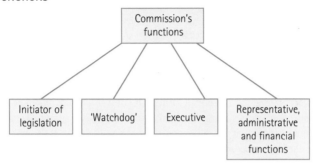

Initiator of EU action

The Commission has historically had the right of legislative initiative, and Council decisions are taken on the basis of Commission proposals. Under Art 225 TFEU (formerly Art 192 EC Treaty), the European Parliament can 'request' a proposal when it considers legislation to be necessary. The Commission does not accept that it must bring forward legislative proposals when faced with such a request. The Commission's function as initiator of changes in policy and legislation is reflected in: the adoption of the annual legislative programme; its monopoly over the power of legislative initiative; and in its competence over financial initiatives.

Under Art 241 TFEU (formerly Art 208 EC Treaty), the Council may request the Commission to undertake any study the Council considers desirable for the attainment of common objectives and to submit to it any appropriate proposals.

Watchdog, i.e. Guardian of the Treaties

The Commission acts as the 'watchdog' of the European Union, either through enforcement proceedings or through its role in competition law.

Articles 258 and 259 TFEU (formerly Articles 226 and 227 EC Treaty): the Commission is in a unique position regarding enforcement proceedings. Under Art 258 and Art 259 proceedings, the Commission can take Member States which are in breach of their Treaties obligations before the Court of Justice

(CJ) . The procedure is in two stages. The first is an informal stage whereby the Commission issues a formal notice and eventually issues a reasoned opinion to the Member State which delimits the nature of the dispute. In practice, the Commission attempts to negotiate a settlement with the Member State, and the majority of cases are settled at the informal stage. The second stage is the formal litigation stage where the Commission takes the errant Member State before the Court of Justice.

Article 259 TFEU proceedings involve one Member State taking another Member State before the Court of Justice (CJ), but even with this procedure the Member State must first take its complaint before the Commission, which will issue a reasoned opinion. In practice, if there is substance to the complaint, then the Commission will take the complaint over. Consequently, Art 259 TFEU is rarely used.

As the Commission is involved in all enforcement proceedings and negotiates the outcome of most such proceedings, it is in a distinctive position. *Snyder* [1993] 56 MLR 19 argues that this enables the Commission to use litigation to develop long term strategies and establish basic principles. For example, in the years prior to the 1 January 1993 deadline for the European internal market, most enforcement proceedings related to the non-implementation of directives. Art 258 TFEU was being used as a tool to ensure the success of the internal market programme.

The Member State is required to comply with the declaratory judgment of the Court of Justice under Art 260(1) TFEU (formerly Art 228(1) TEC). If the Member State fails to comply, then the Commission may take further action against the Member State under Art 260(2) TFEU.

The procedure follows a similar pattern to that under Art 258 TFEU above. The Commission will provide the Member State with an opportunity to submit its observations on the alleged breach, following which the Commission will issue a reasoned opinion requiring the Member State to comply with the Court's judgment within a reasonable period of time. If the Member State does not comply with this reasoned opinion, then the Commission may once again refer the case to the Court of Justice.

However, this time, the Court has the power under Art 260(2) TFEU to impose a financial penalty (either a lump sum payment or a penalty payment) on the Member State for non-compliance with its judgment (e.g. in 1997, the Court imposed a penalty payment of 20,000 € per day on Greece for each day of delay in complying with EU law regarding the disposal of toxic waste).

Competition law: in the past, the Commission had the central role in enforcing EU competition law (e.g. regarding anti-competitive agreements prohibited by Art 101 TFEU (formerly Art 81 TEC) or abuse of a dominant position prohibited by Art 102 TFEU (formerly Art 82 TEC)).

Following enlargement in 2004, a new decentralised system came into place when Regulation 1/2003 came into force. This took the pressure off the Commission, which is now assisted by national competition authorities (NCAs) when enforcing EU competition law. In the UK, the Office of Fair Trading is one of the NCAs.

The Commission may now focus its attention on the more serious breaches of Arts 101 and 102 TFEU (formerly Arts 81 and 82 TEC). Both the Commission and NCAs have the power to impose fines on undertakings which are in breach of EU competition law (e.g. in 2004, the Commission imposed a fine of Euros 497 million on Microsoft). It can, moreover, declare illegal state aids provided by Member States and to bring Member States before the Court of Justice for breaching EU law.

Executive of the Union

The Commission is often called the Executive of the Union. The term is misleading and the Commission's role has fluctuated between a prototype federal government and a secretariat simply carrying out the instructions of the Council of Ministers. The Commission has to ensure that the Union's revenue is collected and passed on by the Member States, to coordinate parts of the Union's expenditures and administering aid to third countries. Since the Lisbon Treaty, the High Representative[1] will present the Union for matters regarding the Common Foreign and Security Policy. The change in role of the Commission has been a response to historical circumstances. Unlike the Parliament, which has seen a steady increase in its powers since the Treaty of Rome, the Commission has seen peaks and troughs in its powers. The key dates are as follows:

[1] The High Representative of the Union for Foreign Affairs and Security Policy is not one of the EU institutions. Its role is to ensure the consistency of the Union's external action as a whole (Art 18 TEU) and to contribute to policy development in the field of common foreign and security policy and common security and defence policy.

1958–65: This period was the high point of the Commission's powers, when it seemed to be evolving into some sort of federal government. It negotiated the elimination of customs tariffs and a common agricultural policy, although it had less success with the establishment of a common external tariff, internal liberalising measures and energy and transport policy.

1966 – Luxembourg Accords: This convention was developed in response to a constitutional crisis in the Community. Where the vital interests of a Member State are at stake, it can veto a legislative proposal. The Community was put on a more inter-governmentalist footing and the Commission took on more of the characteristics of a secretariat.

The status of the Luxembourg Accords was subsequently raised by the Treaty of Amsterdam, from that of a constitutional convention to being enshrined in the Treaty itself. The ECJ will now be able to rule on what constitutes a matter within a Member State's 'vital national interest'.

1974 – Formation of the European Council: This again gave a more inter-governmentalist flavour to the Community.

1986 – Single European Act (SEA): The 1992 deadline enhanced the Commission's role. It became more active in the legislative sphere and in negotiation with national governments.

1992 – Treaty on European Union: The Commission's power was on the wane again. The right of legislative initiative was diluted. The new legislative procedure in Art 294 TFEU (formerly Art 251 TEC) only allows for the Commission to mediate in the Conciliation Committee and its proposals can be amended by a qualified majority. This weakens the Commission, as it makes its proposals easier to change.

1997 – Treaty of Amsterdam: The ToA introduced amendments to the co-decision procedure laid down in Art 294 TFEU (formerly Art 251 of the EC Treaty) which further strengthened the hand of the European Parliament. The Commission is still left with a mediating role in the Conciliation Committee.

However, the European Parliament failed to secure a shared right of legislative initiative with the Commission. The European Parliament had requested at the Inter-Governmental Conference (IGC) which preceded the ToA that the Commission be forced to respond to its requests for legislative proposals, but such a right was not granted.

> **2003 – Treaty of Nice:** The Treaty of Nice opened the way to the institutional reform needed for the EU enlargement with the accession of countries from eastern and southern Europe. The main changes made by the Treaty of Nice relate to limiting the size and composition of the Commission, extending qualified majority voting, a new weighting of votes within the Council and making the strengthened cooperation arrangements more flexible.
>
> **2009 – Treaty of Lisbon:** The co-decision procedure, as provided for in the former Art 251 EC Treaty (now 294 TFEU) is retained largely unchanged, becoming the 'ordinary legislative procedure'. The Treaty also extends the Commission's exclusive right of initiative in some areas. It also strengthens the Commission's role as independent 'referee' in economic governance.

Legislative powers

The Commission has a small, primary legislative power. In *France, Italy and United Kingdom v Commission* [1980], it was held that the Commission had a right to legislate where it is clear from a purposive interpretation of a Treaty provision that it was intended to give such a right to the Commission, e.g. under Art 106(3) TFEU (formerly Art 86(3) TEC).

The Commission has direct legislative powers only in the fields of ensuring that public undertakings comply with the rules contained in the Treaties (Art 106(3) TFEU) and determining the conditions under which EU nationals may reside in another Member State (Art 45(3)(d) TFEU).

The Commission is often involved in the detailed implementation of Council decisions. This frequently involves further legislation and the Commission has been given wide powers of delegated legislation, which is often referred to as 'quasi-legislative powers'. The Council has not relinquished total control over the delegated legislation and retains varying degrees of control.

With the disappearance of the pillar structure the Commission's scope to launch infringement proceedings has been extended to the area of police cooperation and judicial cooperation for criminal matters (subject to a transition period of five years from 1 December 2009).

Recommendations and opinions

The Commission can formulate recommendations or opinions on matters dealt with in the Treaties. It can, since the entering into force of the Lisbon Treaty, issue in some events direct warnings to Member States regarding economic policy areas.

Representative, financial and administrative functions

The Commission has a number of representative, financial and administrative functions:

- it represents the Member States in negotiations with non-Member States;

- it is responsible for the administration of EU funds.

COMPOSITION

Prior to the EU's enlargement in May 2004, there were 20 members of the Commission, appointed by the governments of the Member States. The five biggest states (France, Germany, Italy, Spain and the UK) had two Commissioners and the other States one each. Since the enlargement of the EU the Commission counts 27 Commissioners. Every Member State has one Commissioner regardless of population size or economic strength (in other words, Germany has one Commissioner, as does Malta). This rule has been reaffirmed at the European Council meeting in December 2008. Although the Lisbon Treaty proposed a Commission consisting of a member from 2/3 of the member states from 2014 (according to Art 17(4) TEU), following the Irish rejection of the Lisbon Treaty by referendum on 12 June 2008, a compromise was reached whereby Ireland would agree to hold a second referendum. The compromise with Ireland provides that all Member States retain their Commissioner.

The powers of the European Parliament over the appointment of European Commissioners have been extended by the TEU, the ToA and the Lisbon Treaty. Currently, under Art 17 TEU (formerly Art 214(2) TEC), the European Council, acting by qualified majority, shall propose to the European Parliament a candidate for the Presidency of the Commission. The candidate shall be elected by the Parliament by a majority of its component members.

The Council then, by common accord with the President-elect, shall suggest the people they wish to see serve as Members of the Commission. The president, the High Representative of the Union for Foreign Affairs and Security Policy and the other members of the Commission shall be subject as a body to a vote of consent by the Parliament.

Despite the careful attention to the representation of each Member State, Commissioners are not the representatives of national governments, but they are intended to represent, independently, the interests of the EU as a whole (there is one exception to the principle of independence regarding the High Representative of the European Union for Foreign Affairs and Security Policy[2]).

The Commission is headed by a President who is proposed by the European Council acting by QMV and elected by the Parliament. It further includes Vice Presidents and other Members of the Commission. The President of the Commission is its leader and most prominent member. Art 248 TFEU states that 'the Members of the Commission shall carry out the duties developed upon them by the President under his authority'.

One of the Vice-Presidents shall be, according to Art 18(4) TEU, the High Representative of the Union for Foreign Affairs, who shall ensure the consistency of the Union's external action and who shall be appointed by the European Council with the agreement of the President of the Commission (see Art 18(1) TEU).

The Commission is divided into a number of departments called Directorates-General (DGs). These Directorates-General are responsible for different aspects of EU policy and divided into four groups: policies, external relations, general services and internal services. Commissioners are given responsibility for particular DGs as part of their portfolio. Each DG is headed by a Director General who is responsible to the relevant Commissioner.

---

[2] This is because the High Representative is responsible for the conduct of the EU Common Foreign and Security Policy and is also a member of the Commission.

Directorates-General are sub-divided into Directorates (headed by a Director), and these in turn are made up of Divisions (each under a Head of Division).

Each Commissioner is assisted by a Cabinet, which is a type of private office and regularly consists of 7–8 officials. The Cabinet which is officially appointed by the President acts as an interface between the Commissioner and the DGs. The heads of the Cabinets meet regularly to co-ordinate activities and prepare the ground for Commission meetings. They are led by the EU Commission Secretary General.

Commissioners are appointed for five year renewable terms (Art 17(3) TEU). All the terms expire together, so the whole of the Commission is reappointed at the same time. National governments cannot dismiss a Commissioner during a term of office; they can only fail to renew a term.

The Commission can be forced to resign *en bloc* by the Parliament, but this cannot be used to dismiss individual Commissioners (Art 17(8) TEU and Art 234 TFEU). Individual members of the Commission shall resign if the President so requests (Art 17(6) TEU).

The Court of Justice can compel a Commissioner to retire on grounds of serious misconduct or because he no longer fulfils the conditions required for the performance of his duties.

THE COUNCIL[3]

The purpose of the Council of is to represent the national interest.

FUNCTIONS

Its main functions are to:

- take general policy decisions;

- ensure that objectives set out in the Treaties are attained;

- ensure co-ordination of general economic policies of Member States;

---

[3] The EU Treaties refer to the Council, although some commentators refer to the Council of Ministers.

- take decisions on the adoption of legislation (generally based on Commission proposals);

- frame the Common Foreign and Security Policy and take decisions to define and implement it;

- jointly decide the budget with the Parliament.

COMPOSITION

The Council is not a fixed body and each Member State is represented by a government minister. Which government minister attends the meeting will depend on the subject matter of the meeting. The Member States will be represented by the government minister responsible for that particular specialisation. With the Lisbon Treaty the number of Council meetings, or 'configurations' as they are called, have increased from nine to ten (e.g. Economic and Financial Affairs; Justice and Home Affairs; Employment, Social Policy and Consumer Affairs; Competitiveness; Transport, Telecommunications and Energy; Environment; Agriculture and Fisheries; Education, Youth and Culture). The General Affairs and External relations configuration has been formalised and split into two separate configurations, thereby increasing the number to ten now (with the Lisbon Treaty).

PRESIDENCY

The former Art 203 EC treaty provided for the rotation of the presidency of the Council between the Member States. The overarching rotating Presidency of the Council has been abolished by the Lisbon Treaty and replaced by the team presidencies. Now, all configurations are presided over by one of the Council's Member State representatives on the basis of the system of equal rotation (16(9) TEU). The sole exception is the Foreign Affairs Council, presided over by the High Representative of the Union for Foreign Affairs and Security. The President of a particular configuration chairs the meetings, sets the agenda for them, and also has responsibility to ensure the smooth running of the configuration. This provides an opportunity for Member States to ensure that relevant issues to them are placed at the top of the agenda.

To a large extent, the Presidency will enable a Member State to control the agenda of the European Union, so a Member State will attempt to use the time that it holds the Presidency to push through as many measures as possible.

COREPER

The government ministers who comprise the Council will have full time ministerial responsibilities in their own country, and as a result are only present in Brussels for short periods.

In order to provide continuity, a Committee of Permanent Representatives, known as COREPER (French acronym), was established. This Committee plays a central role in the preparation of Council meetings. COREPER has no power to take formal decisions other than on Council procedures.

Article 240 TFEU provides that the Committee is responsible for preparing the work of the Council and for carrying out the tasks assigned to it.

There are two tiers to COREPER itself. COREPER I, composed of deputy permanent representatives is responsible for social affairs, the internal market and the environment. More sensitive issues, such as economic and financial affairs, are dealt with by the Permanent Representatives themselves, and this is known as COREPER II. Their function is to represent the Member States at a lower level than the Ministers.

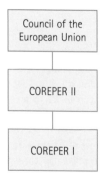

COREPER is assisted by about 250 working groups which examine Commission proposals. In these meetings, a Member State is often represented by a national expert. In the working groups of COREPER the adoption of some 85 per cent of all EU legislation effectively takes place, to be formally approved without discussion at Council meetings.

COREPER has been called a 'mixed' institution, part of a 'grey zone' of institutions which cannot be classified as belonging either to the Union or to Member States.

VOTING

With the Lisbon Treaty, majority voting rather than unanimous decisions will become more common. The new Lisbon Treaty provides in Art 16(3) TEU that 'the Council shall act by a qualified majority except where the Treaties provide otherwise' (re-placing former Art 205(1) TEC).

In practice, only a few unimportant matters are decided by a simple majority. Some matters, for example admission of new members, are decided unanimously. Most matters are decided by a *'qualified majority'*, where the votes of larger States have greater weight than the votes of smaller ones. As provided under former Art 205 TEC (Art 238 TFEU), the votes of the Member States are currently weighted (until 2014) as follows:

France, Germany, Italy, UK	29 votes (each)
Spain, Poland	27 votes (each)
Romania	14 votes
Netherlands	13 votes
Belgium, Czech Republic, Greece, Hungary, Portugal	12 votes (each)
Austria, Bulgaria, Sweden	10 votes (each)
Denmark, Finland, Ireland, Lithuania, Slovakia	7 votes (each)
Cyprus, Estonia, Latvia, Luxembourg, Slovenia	4 votes (each)
Malta	3 votes
Total	345 votes

A qualified majority is 255 votes (representing 73.91 of the total votes). In other words, 91 votes will be needed to block a proposal.

From 1 November 2014, Art 238 TFEU (formerly art 205 TEC) provides for new rules in combination with the protocol for transitional provisions.

The Lisbon Treaty has made significant changes to the system for calculating the qualified majority within the Council and to areas to which it applies. The voting system introduced in the Nice Treaty will continue to apply until 1 November 2014. From November 2014 onwards, qualified-majority voting will be based on the principle of 'double majority', which will be attained when at least 55 per cent of the Member States comprising at least fifteen of them and making up at least 65 per cent of the Union's population (see Art 16(4) and (5) TEU).

'Double Majority'

This procedure requires for a proposal to be adopted that a majority of Member States (i.e. at least 14 out of 27, regardless of size and population) must vote in favour.

'Demographic safety net'

Another rule introduced (in addition to the double majority voting) is the 'demographic safety net'. This means that each Member State can request verification of whether the qualified majority represents at least 62 per cent of the population of the EU. If this condition is not fulfilled, the decision cannot be adopted.

New Development with the Lisbon Treaty

- Formalisation of the General Affairs Council and the External Relations Council.

- New formula of the weighting and thresholds for QMV (Art 16(4) and (5) TEU) (no change before 2014).

EUROPEAN COUNCIL

In 1974, it was agreed that the heads of government of the Member States, together with their foreign ministers, would hold summit conferences at regular intervals. These became known as the 'European Council' and achieved legal status by virtue of Art 2 of the SEA. It comprises the Heads of governments of the Member States, its President and the President of the Commission.

The title 'European Council' is confusing, since it is not the same body as the Council.

The European Council possesses no formal powers. It is an informal forum for discussions relating to issues of common EU concern and is a vehicle for co-ordinating the Member States' foreign policies to ensure that they maximise their influence on world affairs. To this end, the SEA places an obligation 'to endeavour jointly to formulate and implement a European foreign policy'. The Lisbon Treaty has for the first time formally recognised the European Council as an institution. As an official EU institution its acts or its 'failing to act' is now subject to review by the Court of Justice.

Article 15(1) TEU (formerly Art 4 TEU) provides a further role for the European Council when it states that it shall 'provide the Union with the necessary impetus for its development and shall define the general political directions and priorities thereof. It shall not exercise legislative functions.'

The President of the European Council is, after Lisbon, elected by qualified majority voting of its members for a term or two and is renewable once (Art 15(5)–(6) TEU).

EUROPEAN PARLIAMENT

The Parliament was set up as an 'Assembly' and was only formally recognised as the European Parliament in the SEA. Currently, it is composed of 736 Members and seats are not evenly distributed on the basis of population.

Member State MEP allocations for the 2009–2014 European Parliamentary term (as the Parliament was elected before the entry into force of the Lisbon Treaty):

Germany	99
France, UK, Italy	72 (each)
Poland, Spain	50 (each)
Romania	33
Netherlands	25
Belgium, Czech Republic, Greece, Hungary, Portugal	22 (each)
Sweden	18
Austria, Bulgaria	17 (each)
Denmark, Finland, Slovakia	13 (each)
Ireland, Lithuania	12 (each)
Latvia	8
Slovenia	7
Cyprus, Estonia, Luxembourg	6 (each)
Malta	5
Total	**736**

The Lisbon Treaty provides that the number of MEPs shall not exceed 750 plus the President, with a minimum threshold of 6 members per Member State. It was additionally agreed that no Member State should be allocated more than 96 members (Art 14(2) TEU). A unilateral declaration from the December 2008 European Council meeting (as established under Art 14(3) TEU) stated the number of MEPs will increase from 736 to 754 with the entry into force of the Lisbon Treaty. The new allocation will be based on 'degressive proportionality', combining the principle of 'per head' representation and the principle: the larger the population, the lower the weighting per head. The additional 18 MEPs will be elected for the remainder of the 2009–2014 parliamentary term.

POWERS AND DUTIES

The powers and duties of the European Parliament can be categorised as follows:

- supervisory function;

- participation in legislative processes of the Union;

- budgetary function;

- special powers.

SUPERVISORY FUNCTION

The Commission is politically accountable to the Parliament. The Parliament consequently has a number of powers to hold the Commission accountable:

- the Commission has to reply orally or in writing to questions put to it by the Parliament (Art 230 TFEU, formerly Art 197 TEC);

- the Parliament can demand the resignation of the Commission *en bloc* (Arts 17(8) TEU and 234 TFEU);

- the Parliament debates the annual report produced by the Commission (Art 233 TFEU, formerly Art 200 TEC);

- there is a system of Parliamentary Committees which prepare decisions of the Parliament and maintain regular contact with the Commission when the Parliament is not sitting;

- members of the Commission participate in Parliamentary debates;

- the Parliament uses its budgetary powers to hold the Commission accountable.

The Parliament also exercises supervisory powers over the Council. Although not obliged to do so, the Council replies to both written and, through the President of the relevant Council formation, oral questions. Council Presidents are invited to appear before Parliamentary committees and attend plenary sessions to give the views of Council or give an account of Council business. A problem in supervising the Council arises from the fact that it represents the national interest and, therefore, speaks with a discordant voice.

The TEU and the Lisbon Treaty gave additional supervisory powers to the Parliament:

- it has the right to set up temporary Committees of Inquiry to investigate 'alleged contraventions or maladministration in the implementation of Union law' (except where the matter is *sub judice*) (Art 226 TFEU, formerly Art 193 TEC);

- any citizen of the Union or any resident of a Member State has the right to petition the European Parliament on a matter within EU competence which affects him directly (Art 227 TFEU, formerly Art 194 TEC);

☐ an Ombudsman, appointed by the Parliament, is empowered to receive complaints concerning instances of maladministration in the activities of EU institutions or bodies (except the Court of Justice and the General Court) (Art 228 TFEU).

The jurisdiction of the Ombudsman was extended to the reformed third pillar of the European Union, that of Police and Judicial Co-operation in Criminal Matters, by the Treaty of Amsterdam. With the Lisbon Treaty the pillar structure has been abolished and third pillar subjects now fall under the jurisdiction of the Union.

PARTICIPATION IN THE LEGISLATIVE PROCESS

In contrast with national parliaments, the European Parliament has no ability to initiate legislation.

One of the Parliament's main functions has traditionally been to advise and be consulted on proposed legislation. Prior to the SEA, the Treaties gave the European Parliament a right to be consulted only in the legislative process.

Prior to the Lisbon Treaty the most significant area in which legislation could be adopted without any involvement of the European Parliament was that of the common commercial policy. Art 133 TEC simply required a Commission proposal and adoption by the Council, acting by a qualified majority. In practice, the Commission usually suggested that the Parliament be consulted on an optional basis and the Council frequently follows this advice. This has changed with the Lisbon Treaty, which now requires that 'The European Parliament and the Council [. . .] shall adopt the measures defining the framework for implementing the common commercial practice' (Art 207(2) TFEU).

The Parliament's legislative powers vary according to the legislative procedure adopted. There are different legislative procedures in which the European Parliament is involved.

The main procedures are

1) the ordinary procedure (the then co-decision procedure); and
2) the special procedures:
   a) the consultation
   b) the assent.

The relevant procedure and consequently the Parliament's involvement in the process is governed by the Treaties. With the Lisbon Treaty the former co-operation procedure has been abolished and replaced by the use of the ordinary legislative procedure or the special procedures. The variants on the number of decision making procedures have been criticised for creating a lack of transparency. The number of different procedures makes it very difficult for laypersons/citizens to understand how EU law is made and the roles of the three political institutions. The Lisbon Treaty aims at simplifying these procedures.

1. Ordinary legislative procedure [formerly co-decision procedure referred to in former Article 251 TEC now art 289 TFEU]

The ordinary legislative procedure (formerly co-decision procedure) was introduced by the TEU and granted the Parliament greater influence in the law-making process. The ToA streamlined the procedure and further strengthened the Parliament's bargaining powers. However, technically speaking, the Parliament still does not share legislative power equally with the Council. The Parliament has new powers of amendment, but it cannot demand that these amendments are accepted. Ultimately, it has the power to veto a proposal.

The procedure under former Article 251 TEC applies to most legislation approved by the EC. These areas were extended by the ToA, the TN and the Lisbon Treaty. The procedure is now provided for in the Art 294 TFEU and it now extends to the area of freedom, security and justice.

The procedure starts off when the Commission drafts a proposal and sends it to the Council and the Parliament. The Parliament shall adopt its position at *first reading* and communicate it to the Council. If the Council approves the European Parliament's position, the act concerned shall be adopted in the wording which corresponds to the position of the European Parliament. If the Council does not approve the European Parliament's position, it shall adopt its position at first reading and communicate it to the European Parliament. The Council shall inform the European Parliament fully of the reasons which led it to adopt its position at first reading. The Commission shall inform the European Parliament fully of its position.

A *second reading* then takes place before the Parliament. If within three months, the Parliament fails to make a decision or approves the common position, the Council can adopt the act. If the Parliament rejects the common position by majority of its membership, the act is deemed not to be adopted (i.e. the Parliament can veto the proposal). Alternatively, the Parliament can propose amendments by an absolute majority of its component members. The proposals are sent to the Commission and the Council. The Commission shall then deliver an opinion on the proposals.

Within three months the Council may approve the Parliament's amended text and adopt the act (by qualified majority if the Commission has accepted all the amendments, but by unanimity if the Commission has rejected all the amendments).

If the Council fails to agree to the Parliament's proposals, a Conciliation Committee is established which consists of representatives of the Council (acting by qualified majority) and of the Parliament (acting by majority of the members representing it) with the Commission acting as a mediator. If a joint text is not approved by the Committee within six weeks, the proposal is now dropped. If a joint text is approved, the act will be adopted by the Parliament acting by the majority of votes cast and the Council acting by a qualified majority. If either institution fails to adopt the joint text within six weeks, the act will be dropped.

The deadlines of three months and six weeks may be extended by one month and two weeks, respectively, in certain circumstances set out in Article 294 TFEU (formerly Article 251 TEC).

2. Special Procedures
a. Consultation procedure

The Commission forwards a proposal to the Council, which in turn forwards it to the Parliament for its opinion. The proposal is passed to the appropriate Parliamentary Committee before a plenary session of Parliament gives its opinion. There is no obligation on the Commission or the Council to follow this opinion. However, failure to consult the Parliament where there is a Treaty requirement to do so, is a breach of an 'essential procedural requirement' and the legislation will be annulled (*Roquette v Council* [1980] and *Maizena v Council* [1980]).

The Parliament must be re-consulted if the Commission amends the proposal or the Council intends to use its own power of amendment and the resulting text, considered as a whole, differs in substance from the one which was the subject of the original request for an opinion (Case C-65/90 *European Parliament v Council* [1992]).

There is no requirement on the Commission to consult the Parliament while formulating a proposal. However, the Parliament can use its supervisory power over the Commission to indirectly influence the Council in the consultation procedure. The Council takes its decisions on the basis of Commission proposals. The Commission would want its proposals to enjoy broad support from the Parliament, as the former is accountable to the latter. In this indirect way, the Parliament can bring pressure to ensure that its opinions are respected.

Certain provisions of the Treaties require the Council, before taking a decision, to consult, either in addition to or instead of the European Parliament, other EU institutions or bodies. Previously, the only bodies to be consulted were the Economic and Social Committee and the Court of Auditors in relation to financial legislation. The TEU extends the range of bodies from which opinions must be sought. In particular, it provides for a Committee of Regions.

The tendency was to limit the use of the consultation procedure to economic sectors of special political sensitivity in the Member States, or to matters felt to impinge directly on sovereignty.

b. Assent procedure

The assent procedure was introduced by the SEA. Originally, the Parliament's approval was required for the admission of new members and for the conclusion of association agreements. The category of agreements to which it applies was considerably enlarged by the TEU. It applies to more international agreements and, also includes:

- acts defining the tasks, policy objectives and organisation of structural funds;

- the decision to set up a Cohesion Fund;

- various aspects of the functioning of the European Central Bank;

- amendment of certain provisions of the Statute of European System of Central Banks (ESCB).

The Treaty of Lisbon has enhanced this procedure, which now governs significant fields, such as EU anti-discrimination policy (Art 19 TFEU), a significant part of EU criminal justice policy (82, 83(1), (6), 86(1), (4) TFEU).

This procedure is characterised by the fact that the legislative proposal can also be made by the Parliament, Member States or the European Council. The proposal may come directly to the Parliament or other institutions will have to give their consent. The Parliament has to consent to the measure before it can become law.

BUDGETARY POWERS

The Parliament's powers in relation to the budget were significantly increased by the Budgetary Treaties of 1970 and 1975. As a result of the latter Treaty, the

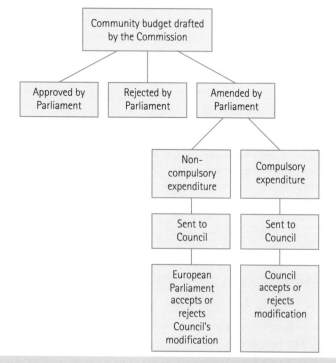

Parliament now jointly exercises control over the budget with the Council, although since 1988 it does so within the context of 'budgetary discipline'. Whilst the Commission sets the budget, which may then be adopted by the Council, the Parliament has the right to veto it.

The budget is drafted by the Commission. The Lisbon Treaty has removed the distinction between compulsory and non-compulsory expenditure, thus giving the European Parliament an influence on all budgetary categories.

PARLIAMENT AND THE COURT OF JUSTICE

Historically, the Parliament has been weak, and it has constantly been attempting to extend its role and increase its power and influence. One method developed by the Parliament to put pressure on the Council to take decisions has been to take cases to the Court of Justice.

Failure to act: In *European Parliament v Council* [1985], the Court held that the Parliament could bring proceedings against the Council under Art 265 TFEU (formerly Art 232 TEC) for failure to act when the Council had been in breach of its Treaty obligations by failing to adopt a common transport policy. Although the Court held that the Council should have acted, it was not prepared to say what the content of the Council's provisions should have been.

Action to annul: Although the right to bring an action for failure to act was granted readily, there was initially far more reluctance on the part of the Court of Justice to allow the Parliament privileged status in bringing actions for the other type of judicial review, that of 'actions to annul' under Art 263 TFEU (formerly Art 230 TEC). A long line of cases, for example, Case 377/87 *European Parliament v Council* [1988] and Case 302/87 *European Parliament v Council (Comitology case)* [1988], held that the European Parliament did not have power to bring annulment proceedings. Eventually, it was held in Case 70/88 *European Parliament v Council (Chernobyl* case) [1990] that the Parliament could bring an action to annul where there had been an infringement of the Parliament's rights and the action was taken in order to safeguard those rights. Article 263 TFEU (formerly Article 230 TEC) was amended by the TEU to reflect this change in standing resulting from the Court's case law. The Parliament was finally granted full standing in the Treaty of Nice and re-affirmed in the Lisbon Treaty.

Actions against Parliament: The Parliament can be a defendant as well as a complainant before the Court of Justice. The original intention of the Treaty drafters was that the Parliament should be liable for its decisions in staff cases. Liability has since been extended and the Court has held that the Parliament can be a source of 'justiciable acts' and can be sued under Art 263 TFEU (formerly Art 230 TEC) (actions to annul). This has led to other EU institutions and individuals (other than staff) challenging the decisions of the European Parliament.

So, in *Parti Ecologiste 'Les Verts' v European Parliament* [1983], a French political party was able to obtain annulment of European Parliament Bureau decisions concerning the distribution of funds to political parties who participated in the 1984 Euro elections.

Similarly, in *Case 34/86 Council v European Parliament* [1986], the Council obtained a ruling that the decision of the President of the Parliament declaring the 1986 budget adopted was illegal.

This does not mean that all acts of the Parliament are 'justiciable'. The reason the Court of Justice included acts of the Parliament within actions to annul was to ensure that all legally binding acts were capable of judicial review. In *Group of the European Right v European Parliament* [1985], a decision by the President of the European Parliament declaring admissible a motion for the setting up of a Committee of Inquiry into the rise of fascism and racism was not capable of challenge.

Historical development of the European Parliament's powers
Examination questions frequently ask for an historical analysis of the development of the European Parliament's powers. It is important to keep certain key dates in mind.

1957 – Founding Treaties: These give the Parliament the right to advise and be consulted, and to supervise the Commission. A small number of special powers are also granted.

1970–75 – Budgetary Treaties: These give the Parliament: power to reject draft budget in its entirety; final say on non-compulsory expenditure; power to propose amendments to compulsory expenditure.

1979 – Direct elections: Not an increase in powers but an enhancement of the Parliament's moral authority which encouraged the Parliament to use existing draconian powers, that is, rejection of draft budget to pressurise other institutions.

1986 – Single European Act: Introduction of co-operation procedure. Assent to new members and association agreements. But greater implementation powers for Commission.

1992 – Treaty on European Union: More consultative powers. Co-operation procedure extended to new fields. Introduction of procedure referred to in Art 189b (now Art 251), 'the co-decision procedure'. Assent extended to new areas including legislative field. Power of veto over appointment of new Commissioners. 'Committees of Inquiry'. Right to 'request' proposals from Commission. Right of citizens of European Union to petition Parliament. Power to appoint Ombudsman. Consultative role in relation to the Foreign and Security and Justice and Home Affairs pillars of the Union.

1997 – Treaty of Amsterdam: This sees a further extension of the European Parliament's powers. Its position in the co-decision procedure is strengthened.

2003 – Treaty of Nice: With this Treaty, Parliament's legislative and supervisory powers are increased and qualified-majority voting is extended to more areas within the Council.

2009 – Treaty of Lisbon: With the Lisbon Treaty the Parliament gained even greater role in the legislative process. The 'ordinary legislative procedure' which affords co-equal legislative power to the Council and the Parliament applies in an increasing number of policy areas. Moreover, the Parliament is granted new veto powers in some areas.

The European Parliament began as a very weak body but has steadily been increasing its powers. Successive Treaties have augmented its powers. Bieber *et al* (1991) 23 CML Rev 767 argue that, although powers were increased by the Single European Act, in some ways, particularly in relation to the decision making process, the overall effect was neutral. As the Parliament has certain 'horizontal' powers over the whole of the Treaty, it was argued that the effect of the Treaty on the Parliament could only be assessed by considering changes in the powers of the other institutions. The increase in the implementing powers of the Commission affected the Parliament, first, as the committee system (whereby the Council retains some measure of control over implementing legislation) affects the Parliament in its supervisory capacity and, secondly, because the committee system weakens the Parliament's budgetary powers.

The Treaty of Lisbon aims at strengthening the European Parliament's legislative powers by extending the co-decision procedure to further policy areas.

Although the Parliament gives the outward appearance of being like any other Parliament, the reality is quite different. Despite being the sole EU institution which has its members elected on a Euro-wide level, sovereignty still has a role to play. There are *pro rata* far fewer MEPs for the larger Member States than the smaller ones. Also the Executive is not sustained in power by having a majority in Parliament as is the case in the UK with the Government of the day having a majority in the House of Commons.

The Parliament has weak supervisory powers over the Council.

THE COURT OF JUSTICE OF THE EUROPEAN UNION

With the Lisbon Treaty, 'the Court of Justice of the European Union shall include the Court of Justice, the General Court and specialised courts' (Art 19 TEU). The Court of First Instance is renamed the General Court.

EUROPEAN COURT OF JUSTICE renamed the COURT OF JUSTICE – (CJ)

Under Art 19 TEU (formerly Art 220 TEC), the function of the Court of Justice (CJ) is to ensure that in the interpretation and application of the Treaties the law is observed.

Composition: judges and Advocates-General

The CJ consists of one judge from each Member State, so presently there are 27 judges. The judges are assisted by eight Advocates-General. The number of Advocates-General may be increased by the Council acting unanimously if the

CJ requests this (Art 252 TFEU). They must be independent and possess the qualifications required for the appointment to the highest judicial office in their respective countries or be jurisconsults of recognised competence. They are appointed by common accord of the governments of the Member States for a term of six years, expiring at intervals of three years, although they may be reappointed. A judge can only be removed during his term if all the judges and Advocates-General are agreed.

The judges elect a President of the CJ from among their number for a renewable term of three years.

The CJ may sit as a Full Court, a 'Grand Chamber' of thirteen judges, or in chambers consisting of three to five judges. The Court sits in plenary session in all cases where an institution or Member State so requests.

The Advocate-General's position is curious to UK lawyers. The role was based on the *commissaire du gouvernement* in the French Conseil d'État. He/she has the same status as a judge and his/her duty is to present an impartial and reasoned opinion on the case, prior to the judges' deliberations. There is a slight resemblance to the *amicus curiae* in English law. An *amicus curiae* is a 'friend of the court' who gives the court the benefit of his views on a question of law. A major difference between the two is that the Advocate-General, in contrast to the *amicus curiae,* does not represent a particular interest and is completely independent. An opinion is usually, but not always, followed by the Court, and it has no legal force. The Advocate-General can only hope to influence the Court through the force of his/her judgment, as he/she does not take part in the judges' deliberations.

Procedure

Procedure before the CJ has four stages (although the second is often omitted):

1   written proceedings;
2   investigation or preparatory inquiry;
3   oral proceedings;
4   judgment.

Proceedings are commenced by written application. The application can be in any of the official or working languages of the Union. If the applicant is a Member State or individual, the general rule is that the applicant has the choice of language. If the action is against a Member State, the defendant chooses the language of the case. French is the working language of the Court.

The defendant serves a defence in reply to the application, and it is possible for the applicant to serve a reply.

One of the judges is assigned the role of judge *rapporteur* and will study the papers relating to the case, which will also have been examined by the Advocate-General assigned to the case. After close of pleadings the CJ may decide that a preliminary inquiry is needed. Although this is rare, the decision will be based on the judge *rapporteur*'s preliminary report and the views of the Advocate-General.

Prior to the oral hearing, the judge *rapporteur* issues a report summarising the facts of the case and the parties' arguments. During the oral proceedings, counsel for the parties may make submissions to the Court. It has become more common in recent years for the Court to ask legal representatives questions to clarify certain points. The Opinion of the Advocate-General will be delivered and there may be a hearing of any witnesses or experts.

Only one judgment is produced after the judge *rapporteur* has produced another report on the law relating to the case. Deliberations are in secret and the requirement to produce one judgment means that it is often ambiguous where there has been disagreement between the judges, as it has to be sufficiently vague to promote agreement between all the judges. Judgments also tend to be bland, for linguistic reasons.

The Court is bound to include in its judgment a decision as to costs. The usual rule is that the losing party must pay the winning party's costs, but there can be exceptions such as staff cases, where the employer normally pays. Costs in preliminary references are normally reserved to the national court.

The Court can also grant legal aid. It will do so where it seems just and equitable to do so and it can be granted even where it would not be available in national proceedings.

Jurisdiction

The jurisdiction of the ECJ has been conferred on it by the Treaties as follows:

- Action for annulment/judicial review of a EU Institution's acts.

Article 263 TFEU (formerly Art 230 TEC) gives Member States, the Commission, the Council and the European Parliament, *locus standi* to seek judicial review by the CJ of 'acts of the Council, of the Commission and of the ECB, other than recommendations and opinions, and of acts of the European Parliament and the European Council intended to produce legal effects vis-à-vis third parties'. The CJ has given the term 'act' a wide interpretation and it includes all acts intended to have legal effects: *ERTA* [1971].

There are specific grounds on which such judicial review may be sought: lack of competence; infringement of an essential procedural requirement; infringement of the Treaties; or of any other rule of law relating to their application, or misuse of powers. Actions for annulment must be brought within two months of the publication of the act, or its notification to the claimant.

Natural and legal persons (also called individual or non-privileged applicants) have *locus standi* to such judicial review before the Court of Justice but in limited circumstances only, as set out in Art 263(4) TFEU (formerly Art 230(4) TEC). They may challenge:

- an act addressed to them;

- an act addressed to another person which is of direct and individual concern to them;

- a regulatory act which is of direct concern to them and does not entail implementing measures.

An act in the form of a regulation
The aim of this provision was to prevent the EU institutions framing legislation as Regulations in order to prevent judicial review by an individual. The then ECJ's original view was that true regulations could not be challenged: *Calpak v Commission* [1980]. Nevertheless, the Court will consider the nature and content of the challenged act and not its form. The distinguishing factor is whether the measure is of general application. However, with regard to anti-dumping, the then ECJ adopted a more liberal approach and allowed legislative measures in the form of Regulations addressed to Member States to be challenged by individual traders with direct and individual concern. This may be explained by the fact that in the field of anti-dumping, the Commission is only permitted to act by Regulations addressed to Member States and not by

Decisions: *Allied Corporation* [1984]; *Timex* [1985]; *Extramet* [1991]. A similar approach has been adopted in the field of state aid (*COFAZ* [1986]) and competition law (*Metro* [1977]).

This more liberal approach was taken in an agriculture case called *Codorníu* [1994], where the then ECJ allowed a true regulation to be challenged. Codorníu was a Spanish producer of sparkling wine and had used the term 'Gran Crèmant' as a trademark in Spain since the 1920s. In 1989, a Council Regulation was enacted which only permitted the use of the term 'crèmant' by producers of certain sparkling wines in France and Luxembourg. Codorníu sought judicial review under Art 263 TFEU (formerly Art 230 TEC) and successfully challenged the Regulation.

▶ CODORNÍU [1994]

A Spanish producer of sparkling wine sought judicial review of a true Regulation which prevented it from using the term 'Gran Crèmant' to describe its products and which it had used as a trademark in Spain since 1924.

Codorníu successfully challenged the Regulation since it was able to show the then ECJ that it was in a position in which it could be differentiated from all other traders by being deprived of its right to the trademark.

It was thought that this judgment was to signify a change in approach more generally on the part of the Court. However, this change has not materialised in later cases: *Greenpeace and others v Commission* [1995].

Direct concern

An individual applicant cannot challenge a decision (or decision in the form of a Regulation) addressed to another person unless it can show that it is of direct concern to them. This means that there must be a direct causal link between the challenged measure and its ultimate impact on the applicant. The test is whether there is any scope for the exercise of discretion on the part of the addressee (normally a Member State). If so, the applicant will fail the test: *Alcan* [1970]; *Bock* [1971].

Prior to the entry into force of the Lisbon Treaty an individual applicant was not able to challenge a decision (or decision in the form of a Regulation) addressed to another person unless he/she could show that it is of individual concern to them. This requirement has been strictly construed by the Court. The first interpretation took place in the *Plaumann* [1963] case. Plaumann, an importer of clementines into Germany, sought an amendment of a Commission decision addressed to Germany which refused to give Germany authorisation for the partial suspension of customs duties on clementines imported from third countries. The then ECJ held that Plaumann could not challenge the decision addressed to Germany for lack of individual concern. The Court held that:

> 'Persons other than those to whom a Decision is addressed may only claim to be individually concerned if that Decision affects them by reason of certain attributes which are peculiar to them or by reason of circumstances in which they are differentiated from all other persons and by virtue of these factors distinguishes them individually just as in the case of the person addressed.'

The Court added that Plaumann did not satisfy the requirement of individual concern simply by being engaged as an importer of clementines since any person at any time could engage in this particular commercial activity.

Reform

The CJ's approach to the standing of individual applicants has been consistently criticised by academics as being too restrictive. In *Union des Pequenos Agricultores (UPA) v Council* [2002], Advocate-General Jacobs questioned the Court's approach and put forward an alternative test. He argued that:

> Individuals should 'be regarded as individually concerned where, by reason of his particular circumstances, the measure has, or is liable to have a substantial adverse effect on his interests' (para 60).

Before the CJ (then ECJ) delivered its decision in *UPA,* the General Court (formerly CFI) followed the Advocate-General's lead and adopted a more generous approach in its *Jégo-Quéré SA v Commission* [2002] decision. The General

Court held that a measure will have individual concern if it affects the applicant's legal position, '. . . in a manner which is both definite and immediate, by restricting his rights or imposing obligations on him. The number and position of other persons who are likewise affected by the measure, or who may be so, are of no relevance in that regard' (para 51).

When delivering its decision in *UPA*, the Court of Justice did not follow the more liberal test proposed by Advocate-General Jacobs in his Opinion and reverted to its restrictive *Plaumann* test (see above). When the General Court's decision in *Jégo-Quéré* was appealed to the CJ by the Commission, the Court followed its *UPA* decision and overturned the decision of the General Court ruling that it had erred in law: *Commission v Jégo-Quéré* [2004].

The Constitutional Treaty amended former Art 230(4) EC with regard to individual applicants. This amendment was also inserted into the Lisbon Treaty (Art 263 TFEU).

The need to distinguish between a Decision and a Regulation in the form of a Decision has been removed. In addition, individual concern will not need to be shown for regulatory acts which are of direct concern and do not entail implementing measures.

Other actions against Union institutions include:

- Actions for failure to act (Art 265 TFEU, formerly Art 232 TEC), actions for damages (Arts 268 and 340 TFEU, formerly Arts 235 and 288 TEC) and, at one time, staff cases, which are now dealt with by the General Court.

- Preliminary rulings under Art 267 TFEU (formerly Art 234 TEC) (see Chapter 4).

- Actions brought either by the Commission (Art 258 TFEU, formerly Art 226 TEC) or a Member State (Art 259 TFEU formerly Art 227 TEC) against another Member State for failure to fulfil obligations under the Treaties.

- Since 1989, the CJ has had an appellate jurisdiction and hears appeals from the General Court on points of law from undertakings which have been fined as a result of Commission decisions relating to competition law.

- The Court can also give advisory opinions under Art 218 TFEU (formerly Art 300 TEC) on an agreement between the European Union and third countries or international organisations.

Quasi-legislative role

One of the striking features of the CJ is its approach to interpretation. The CJ employs a purposive, or teleological, approach and interprets legislation in accordance with the aims and purpose of the Treaty. In this approach, the Court is guided by the principle of *effet utile*, or effectiveness, and is constantly striving to ensure that its interpretation leads to a furthering of the integration process by ensuring that the European legal order functions more effectively. It is argued that, as a result, the judges are not being creative at all; they are precluded from performing a legislative function, as they are tied to the aims of the Treaties and are, therefore, limited in their policy choices. A problem with this analysis is that there is no unanimous agreement between the Member States as to the form European integration, and consequently the policy choices, should take.

The teleological approach has had several important consequences. First, it has lead to a constitutionalisation of the founding Treaties. This constitution is said to rest on the 'twin pillars' of direct effect and supremacy. (See Chapter 2.)

The CJ has defined the powers of the respective institutions and the competence of the Union. In *Commission v Council* (*ERTA* case) [1971], it was held that the Community (now Union) had competence to enter into an agreement with third countries when policy making in a certain area has been handed over to the Union.

The principle of *effet utile* in combination with Art 4 TEU (formerly Art 10 TEC), under which Member States agree to fulfil their Union obligations, have been used by the CJ to develop an interpretive obligation on Member States (*Von Colson and Kamman* [1986] and *Marleasing* [1990]) and to develop the safeguarding of rights through the availability of compensation in the event of the State breaching those rights (*Francovich* [1990]). (See Chapter 2.)

Easson feels that the activist stage of the CJ has come to an end and, now that the general principles of the legal order are established, further developments will depend on the legislators ('Legal approaches to European integration' (1986)). On the other hand, Ramussen, in *On Law and Policy in the European Court of Justice* (1986), feels that the CJ has been unnecessarily activist in the past and will continue to be so in the future. Rasmussen and Snyder (*Effectiveness of EC law: institutions, processes, tools and techniques* (1993)) see a danger in the Court's activist role, as it lacks legitimacy to perform such a role and there has been a lack of popular involvement in the development of the legal order.

THE GENERAL COURT

The case-load of the CJ has increased dramatically since the inception of the Community. It can now take over two years to receive a judgment. To help alleviate the workload, the Single European Act 1986 provided for the establishment of a General Court (formerly CFI). The General Court was established by Council Decision 88/591 and began hearing cases in 1989.

The General Court consists of 27 judges (at least one judge per Member State, Art 20 TEU) and sits in chambers of three or five judges, or occasionally as a single judge. It may also sit as a 'Grand Chamber' or a Full Court. Article 254 TFEU (formerly Article 225 TEC) provides that, to qualify as judges, 'members of [the] court shall be chosen from persons whose independence is beyond doubt and who possess the ability required for appointment to high judicial office' and they shall be appointed for a period of six years. There is a President of the Court who is elected from amongst the members. There are currently no Advocates-General, but a judge may be asked to undertake this task if the case so requires and the Statute of the CJ can provide for the General Court to be assisted by Advocates-General. The General Court has its own Registry and the members of the court have their own personal staff. All other services are provided by the staff of the CJ and the General Court is 'attached' to the CJ.

The General Court's jurisdiction is as follows:

- staff cases;

- actions brought by natural and legal persons against an EU institution under Arts 263 and 265 TFEU (formerly Arts 230 and 232 TEC) relating to the implementation of competition rules applicable to undertakings;

- all claims brought by 'natural and legal persons' under Arts 263 and 265 TFEU (formerly Arts 230 and 232 TEC) (including anti-dumping cases);

- since the entry into force of the Treaty of Nice, the General Court has jurisdiction to hear preliminary rulings. See Chapter 4.

The competition and staff cases take up most of the General Court's time. Both types of case are fact-based, and were, therefore, thought suitable to transfer to a different court, as they would be the most likely to alleviate the workload of the CJ.

It is possible to appeal a decision of the General Court to the CJ, on points of law only, on three grounds:

1 lack of competence of the General Court;
2 breach of procedure before the General Court which adversely affects the interests of the applicant;
3 infringement of EU law by the General Court.

If the CJ finds that an appeal is successful, it quashes the General Court's judgment. It can then give final judgment itself or refer the case back to the General Court for judgment.

SPECIALISED COURTS (Art 257 TFEU) (formerly Judicial Panels Art 225 a TEC)

The Nice Treaty provided for the establishment by the Council of specialised judicial panels by the European Parliament and the Council which are not with the Lisbon treaty, renamed specialised courts. The aim is to further relieve the burden of work on the Court of Justice and General Court. Decisions given by the specialised courts may be subject to a right to appeal before the General Court on points of law only, exceptionally on matters of facts. The Council created the European Union Civil Service Tribunal in 2004 which hears approximately 150 cases a year dealing with disputes involving employees of the European Union institutions.

You should now be confident that you would be able to tick all of the boxes on the checklist at the beginning of this chapter. To check your knowledge of EU institutions why not visit the companion website and take the Multiple Choice Question test. Check your understanding of the terms and vocabulary used in this chapter with the flashcard glossary.

4

Preliminary rulings

Explain the main purposes of the preliminary reference procedure ☐

Discuss how the procedure has been used to develop EU law ☐

Understand what is meant by 'a court or tribunal' in this context ☐

Distinguish between when a court has a discretion to make a preliminary reference and when it has an obligation to refer ☐

Identify when a preliminary reference would not be necessary ☐

Consider whether the Court of Justice (CJ – formerly ECJ) can refuse to hear a reference ☐

Explain the effect of a preliminary ruling ☐

Outline proposals for reform of the preliminary reference procedure ☐

PRELIMINARY REFERENCES

Article 267 TFEU (formerly Article 234 TEC) gives the Court of Justice (CJ – formerly ECJ) jurisdiction to give preliminary references on questions of interpretation and validity of EU law at the request of the national courts of a Member State. The procedure is a court to court procedure in which the national court is to hear the case, and when it encounters problems relating to interpretation of the Treaties or the interpretation or validity of acts of the institutions of the Union (e.g. regulations, directives, decisions, opinions and recommendations), the case is referred to the Court of Justice. It should be stressed that the validity of the Treaties cannot be questioned. After a ruling, the Court of Justice returns the case to the national court for it to be applied to the facts of the case. So, the case starts and ends in the national courts. Article 267(2) TFEU (formerly Art 234(2) TEC) provides that 'any court or tribunal' has a discretion to request a preliminary reference, but a court against whose decision there is no judicial remedy is obliged to make a preliminary reference under Art 267(3) TFEU (formerly Art 234(3) TEC).

PURPOSE OF PRELIMINARY REFERENCES

There are four main purposes of preliminary references:

1. Uniformity and consistency of interpretation throughout Member States

The principle of supremacy ensures that EU law prevails over national law where the two conflict. This principle would be undermined if the national courts were free to interpret EU law in their own way with the inevitable result that the law would differ from State to State. Preliminary references ensure that there is an authoritative source for interpretation. Although it is possible for secondary legislation to be annulled, preliminary references ensure that only the CJ can do this, again to avoid discrepancies from State to State. The Court interprets its powers more broadly including anything that forms part of the EU legal order, even if it is neither a provision of the Treaties nor a piece of secondary legislation, even though Art 267 TFEU only gives the Court power to give rulings on the Treaties and acts of the EU institutions.

2. Familiarise national courts with workings of European legal order

This has influenced the Court of Justice's approach to requests for references. In the early days, the Court of Justice was keen to encourage requests, as without them it would be unable to develop the legal order. Consequently, the CJ initially was not formalistic in its approach and did not make specifications about the timing or the form of the request. The CJ also emphasised that the process involved an equal division of labour, and that it was not higher in any hierarchy to the national court but was performing an equal but different role alongside the national courts. This approach was successful and the Court currently has a large backlog of requests.

It has been argued by Craig and de Búrca, *EU Law: Text, Cases and Materials*, 4th edition, Oxford: OUP, 2007, that in recent years, the relationship has become more hierarchical in nature.

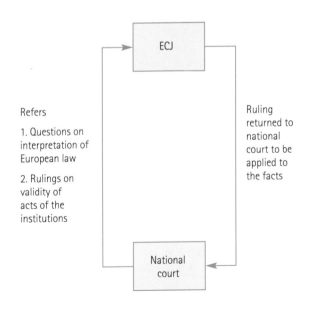

Refers

1. Questions on interpretation of European law

2. Rulings on validity of acts of the institutions

ECJ

Ruling returned to national court to be applied to the facts

National court

3. Develop EU law

The CJ has used preliminary references to develop the legal order and to constitutionalise the Treaties. So, it was through requests for preliminary references that the CJ was able to develop the 'twin pillars' of direct effect (*Van Gend en Loos* [1963]) and supremacy (*Costa v ENEL* [1964]).

The CJ has also been able to extend the scope and effectiveness of the legal order through a combination of preliminary references and Art 4(3) TEU (formerly Art 10 TEC). In this way, it has created an interpretive obligation on Member States to ensure that national courts interpret national legislation in accordance with the aims and purposes of directives (*Von Colson and Kamman* [1984]; *Marleasing* [1992]); individuals receive compensation where they have suffered damage as a result of a Member State breaching its EU obligations (*Francovich* [1992]); and there are effective procedural remedies to ensure the protection of EU rights (*Factortame* [1990]).

4. Rulings on direct effect

Preliminary references have also been used to determine whether Treaty provisions and secondary legislation satisfy the criteria for direct effect and can consequently be relied upon by individuals before national courts.

WHAT IS A COURT OR TRIBUNAL?

Article 267 TFEU (formerly Article 234 TEC) permits only references from a 'court or tribunal'. Essentially, the test for 'court or tribunal' is a wide one and includes any body with official backing which exercises a judicial function according to the normal rules of adversarial procedure and has the power to give binding determinations of legal rights and obligations, independent of the parties in dispute (*Dorsch Consult* [1997]). It is not decisive that the body is recognised as a court under national law (*Corbiau* [1993]).

In (*Cartesio* [2008]) the Court ruled that a body must be independent, be established by law and have a compulsory jurisdiction, and be taking decisions of a judicial nature to be considered as a court. In *Nederlandse Spoorwegen* [1973], the Dutch Raad van State was held to be a court or tribunal within the meaning of Art 267 TFEU (formerly Art 234 TEC). In theory, an application for judicial review in the Netherlands is decided by the Crown but is in practice based on the advice of the Raad van State. The CJ took a pragmatic view and found that the Raad van State was a court or tribunal within Art 267 TFEU (formerly Art 234 TEC).

In *Vassen* [1966], a reference from a body which was an arbitration tribunal but whose members were appointed by the Dutch Minister for Social Security and operated in accordance with ordinary adversarial procedure did come within Art 267 TFEU (formerly Art 234 TEC).

Similarly, in *Broekmeulen* [1981], a Dutch body called the Appeals Committee for General Medicine heard appeals from a medical disciplinary tribunal. The ability to practise as a medical practitioner was dependent on registration with the Committee and one-third of the Appeals Committee's members were appointed by the Dutch Government. This too was held to be a 'court or tribunal' within the meaning of Art 267 TFEU (formerly Art 234 TEC).

A tribunal which mixes judicial functions with other functions was still held to be a tribunal within the meaning of Art 267 TFEU (formerly Art 234 TEC) in *Pretore di Salo v Persons Unknown* [1987].

The Court of Justice will accept requests for references from any body satisfying the criteria, regardless of whether or not the body bears the name 'court' or 'tribunal'. Thus, reference requests have been accepted from Italy's Bar Council (*Gebhard* [1996]), Sweden's Universities' Appeals Board (*Abrahamsson & Anderson v Fogelqvist* [2000]) and the UK's Immigration Adjudicator (*El-Yassini* [1999] and *Kaba* [2000]) and Social Security Commissioner (*O'Flynn* [1996]).

In *De coster v College des Bourgmestres et Echevins de Watermael-Boitsfort* [2000], the Court of Justice stated that when determining whether a body is a court or tribunal 'the court takes account of a number of factors, such as whether the body is established by law, whether it is permanent, whether its jurisdiction is compulsory, whether its procedure is inter partes, whether it applies rules of law and whether it is independent'.

Lack of jurisdiction

A commercial arbitration tribunal was held not to come within Art 267 TFEU (formerly Art 234 TEC) in *Nordsee v Reederei Mond* [1982], and this rule applies even if the award of the tribunal can be enforced through the courts.

The Court of Justice also refused to accept requests for references from a public prosecutor in *Criminal Proceedings against X* [1996] – a prosecutor clearly does not exercise judicial functions – and from the Swedish revenue board in *Victoria Film* [1998], on the basis that its functions were purely administrative with no powers to resolve legal disputes.

WHEN TO REFER

The question of the national court's timing of a reference is dependent on the distinction of Art 267(2) and (3) TFEU (obligatory or discretionary) and can only be understood in the context of the Court of Justice's changing policy in relation to preliminary references. In the initial stages, the CJ was keen to encourage references, as without them it would be unable to familiarise national courts with their approach and develop the legal order. Emphasis was placed on the co-operative aspects of the procedure and the fact that there was an equal division of labour between the CJ and the national court. As a result of this policy, the Court was relaxed about the timing of references. Similarly, it has not been formalistic in its approach and, in the past, if the question had not been properly asked, the Court of Justice reformulated the question and asked itself the question that should have been asked.

In *R v Henn and Darby* [1981], the Court said that it was preferable but not essential for the facts of a case to be decided prior to a reference. The reason for its preference was that it wished to consider as many aspects of the case as possible before giving its ruling.

In *Creamery Milk Suppliers* [1980], the Irish High Court requested a ruling without first considering the facts. The Court of Justice accepted the reference and said that the timing of the reference was entirely at the national court's discretion.

The Court of Justice became a victim of its success over the working of this co-operative policy. It has developed a backlog of cases and in 2009 the period between the time the reference is made and the adoption of a judgement by the court was on average 17.1 months (see *Annual Report of the ECJ 2009*). There is additionally the period following in which the matter must wait to go back before the national courts and in which the national courts must manage the parties' rights through the grant of interim relief. Due to the caseload and lengthy periods the Court of Justice no longer feels the need to encourage national courts to make references, and in recent cases it has been prepared to take a firmer line on the timing of references.

In both *Pretore di Genova v Banchero* [1993] and *Telemarsicabruzzo SpA v Circostel* [1993], the then ECJ held that the national court must define the factual and legal framework in which the questions arise before making a preliminary reference.

In both cases, the Court said that the questions referred were so vague that they could not be answered. In both cases, it emphasised its role in Art 267 TFEU (formerly Art 234 TEC) proceedings, which is to provide a ruling that would be useful to a national court in the administration of justice. As both cases involved competition law, the facts were particularly complicated, and this heightened the need for a clear description of the facts.

In December 1996, a *Note for Guidance on References by National Courts for Preliminary Rulings* was published by the Court of Justice. The Note is for guidance only and has no binding or interpretative effect.

In the Note, it is said that the order for reference should contain a statement of reasons which is succinct but sufficiently complete to give the Court of Justice, and those to whom it must be notified, a clear understanding of the factual and legal context of the main proceedings.

In particular, it should include:

- a statement of the facts which are essential to a full understanding of the legal significance of the main proceedings;

- an exposition of the national law which may be applicable;

- a statement of the reasons which have prompted the national court to refer the question or questions to the Court of Justice; and

- where appropriate, a summary of the arguments of the parties.

The aim should be to put the Court of Justice in a position to give the national court an answer which will be of assistance to it.

The Court issued a revised Note in 2005 regarding the point in national proceedings when a preliminary reference should be made. It stated 'A national court or tribunal may refer a question to the Court of Justice for a preliminary ruling as soon as it finds that a ruling on the point or points of interpretation or validity is necessary to enable it to give judgment; it is the national court which is in the best position to decide at what stage of the proceedings such a question should be referred.' The Note continued that 'a decision to seek a preliminary ruling should be taken when the proceedings have reached a stage at which the national court is able to define the factual and legal context of the question, so that the Court has available to it all the information necessary to check, where appropriate that Community law applies to the main proceedings'. It may also be in the interests of justice to refer a question for a preliminary ruling only after both sides have been heard.

DISCRETION TO REFER

Under Art 267(2) TFEU (formerly Art 234(2) TEC), any court or tribunal of a Member State has discretion to make a reference to the Court of Justice. This right cannot be curtailed by national law: *Second Rheinmühlen Case* [1974], and it cannot be fettered by a regulation of the EU: *BRT-Sabam* [1974].

Principles under which a British court should exercise its discretion were originally indicated by Lord Denning MR in *Bulmer v Bollinger* [1974]:

- The decision must be necessary to enable the English court to give judgment.

- In deciding whether the reference is necessary, account must be taken of the following factors:

  - Is the answer to the question conclusive of the case?

  - Is there a previous ruling by the CJ on the issue?

  - Is the provision *acte clair*? (see below)

  - Have the facts of the case been decided?

If the court decides that a decision is necessary, it must still consider the following factors:

- delay;

- the difficulty and importance of the point;

- expense;

- the burden on the Court of Justice;

- the wishes of the parties;

- difficulty in framing the question in sufficiently clear terms to benefit from a ruling.

These criteria have been attacked on the grounds that they are unduly restrictive and delaying, because the expense and burden on the parties may, in fact, increase if a referral has to be made by a higher court.

The current approach was set out by Sir Thomas Bingham MR in *R v International Stock Exchange of the UK and the Republic of Ireland ex p Else* [1993]. In his view, three steps need to be taken in deciding whether to make a referral:

- first, find the facts;

- secondly, consider whether the EU law provision is critical to the outcome;

- thirdly, consider whether the court could resolve the provision of EU law with complete confidence.

In addition, the court must be mindful of four factors when making its decision:

- the differences between national law and EU law;

- the pitfalls of entering into an unfamiliar field;

- the need for uniform interpretation;

- the advantage enjoyed by the Court of Justice in interpreting EU legislation.

It was held in *Trent Taverns Ltd v Sykes* [1999] that the Court of Appeal could, in the exercise of its discretion, make a reference to the Court of Justice in a case where the relevant point of Union law had already been decided by the Court of Appeal, as the ordinary principles of *stare decisis* were not applicable to such references.

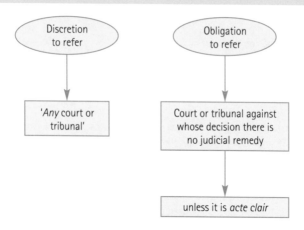

OBLIGATION TO REFER

Article 267(3) TFEU (formerly Article 234(3) TEC) provides that a court or tribunal against whose decision there is no judicial remedy is obliged to make a reference to the Court of Justice. There are two differing views as to what is meant by the phrase 'a court or tribunal against whose decision there is no judicial remedy':

1   'Abstract theory': it can only mean the highest court in the land. In the UK, this would be the House of Lords only. This view was supported by Lord Denning in *Bulmer v Bollinger*.
2   'Concrete theory': it includes courts which are judging in final instance in that particular case. For example, in order to appeal from the Court of Appeal to the House of Lords it is necessary to have leave. If leave is not forthcoming, then the Court of Appeal is the highest court in that particular case. There are comments supporting this theory in *Costa v ENEL* [1964]. In *Hagen* [1980], the Court of Appeal held that it is bound to make a reference under Art 267 TFEU (formerly Art 234 TEC) if leave to appeal to the House of Lords is not obtainable.

However, in *Kenny Roland Lyckeskog* [2000], a Swedish district court asked the CJ whether it had an obligation to refer as an appeal from its decision to the Swedish Supreme Court would only be made if the Swedish Supreme Court stated that such an appeal was admissible. The CJ held that the possibility of an appeal to the Supreme Court meant that the district court could not be considered a court of last resort for the purposes of Art 267 TFEU (formerly Art 234 TEC).

In these circumstances, it seems that the English Court of Appeal would not be considered to be a court 'against whose decisions there is no judicial remedy'.

In theory, the Commission can bring enforcement proceedings against a Member State whose highest court does not make a preliminary reference, but in practice it does not do so.

Interim proceedings

In *Hoffman-La Roche v Centrafarm* [1978], the question arose as to whether an interim order, given in interlocutory proceedings against which there was no judicial remedy but which could be considered again in the main proceedings, was a decision against which there was no judicial remedy. The CJ emphasised that preliminary references could be made but that there was no obligation to make a reference when the matter could be considered again in the main proceedings.

Acte clair

The Court of Justice has sanctioned the use of *acte clair* from French law, subject to conditions, where the answer to the question is clear and free from doubt. If an act is *acte clair*, even a court that comes within Art 267(3) TFEU (formerly Art 234(3) TEC) is freed from its obligation to refer.

In *CILFIT* [1982], the doctrine of *acte clair* was accepted by the Court of Justice, when it said that an application would not be 'necessary' if:

- the question of EU law was irrelevant;

- the provision had already been interpreted by the Court of Justice;

- the correct application is so obvious that it leaves no room for doubt.

In addition to these criteria, the national court must also be convinced that the answer would be equally obvious to a court in another Member State as well as to the Court of Justice. The national court must compare the different versions of the text in the various EU languages. It must also bear in mind that legal concepts and terminology do not necessarily have the same meaning in EU law as in national law.

These last criteria deprive the doctrine of *acte clair* of much of its practical effect. The national judge must not only be satisfied that the provision is free from doubt in his own language but he must peruse the text in the other official languages of the EU and, taking into account the different legal concepts in the different jurisdictions, still be satisfied that the matter is free from doubt. This is an immense challenge, even for the most accomplished linguist. This challenge became even more daunting in May 2004 when 10 new Member States joined the EU, bringing with them several new official languages (Czech, Estonian, Hungarian, Latvian, Lithuanian, Maltese, Polish, Slovak and Slovene). In fact, it is difficult to see how any conscientious judge in the expanded EU could ever honestly conclude that a provision in EU legislation bore the same meaning when read by judges in 27 countries using 22 different languages. The narrowness with which the doctrine has been drawn is a reflection of the advantage that the Court of Justice has over national courts in interpreting legislation and comparing the different texts.

> ### ▶ CILFIT (Case 283/81)
>
> **It was alleged that duties imposed by Italian law were contrary to an EU regulation. The Italian Ministry of Health urged the Italian court against whose decision there was no judicial remedy not to refer the matter to the then CJ as the answer to the question to be referred was obvious.**
>
> **The Court of Justice stated that it may not be necessary to make a reference where the question of EC law is irrelevant, where the question has already been interpreted by the Court and where the correct interpretation is obvious (an *acte clair*).**

It was held in *Da Costa* [1963] that a national court is free to make another preliminary reference, even where the question has been the subject of a previous ruling or where it is *acte clair*.

Validity

In *Foto-Frost* [1987], it was held by the Court of Justice that national courts could not find Community legislation invalid. So the *acte clair* doctrine cannot apply to questions of invalidity, but it is possible for national courts to find

EU acts valid. An exception exists in cases of interlocutory proceedings, where national courts, for reasons of urgency, can rule that Community acts are invalid on an interim basis. In *Zuckerfabrik Süderdithmarschen AG v Hauptzollamt Itzehoe* [1991], it was held that a Community act could be declared temporarily invalid.

The Court of Justice will not overrule a provision of national law in a preliminary reference, but it can say that a rule of national law is inapplicable in an EU context by providing guidance on the correct interpretation of EU law.

Can the Court of Justice refuse to hear a reference?

In recent years, this has been one of the most vexed questions in relation to preliminary references and is a popular topic with examiners.

The Court of Justice will decline to hear a reference when it falls outside Art 267 TFEU (formerly Art 234 TEC), e.g. where the reference is not made by a court or tribunal, as in *Nordsee* [1982], *Criminal Proceedings Against X* [1996] and *Victoria Film* [1998].

If the reference is nothing to do with EU law, the Court of Justice will decline the reference: *Alderblum* [1975]. The fact that the reference has nothing to do with EU law does not mean that it will have been without merit. The national judge will be free to apply national law safe in the knowledge that EU law is not relevant.

Absence of genuine dispute

In *Foglia v Novello (No 1)* [1980], the questions referred concerned an import tax imposed by the French on the import of wine from Italy. The litigation was between two Italian parties. Foglia was a wine producer who agreed to sell wine to Novello, an exporter. In order to challenge the French tax, a clause was inserted into the contract that Foglia would not have to pay any duties levied by the French authorities, which was in contravention of Community law. The parties were agreed that the tax was illegal and the contractual clause was a device to ensure that the matter could be brought before a court.

The Court of Justice refused to hear a reference from the Italian court. It felt that an Italian court was attempting to challenge a French tax and this was abusing the preliminary reference procedure, as it was an indirect method of bringing enforcement proceedings. The Court declined to hear the reference on the grounds that there was an absence of a genuine dispute between the parties. The case was returned to the Italian court and the judge reformulated the questions and referred the matter again to the Court of Justice, which again refused to hear the case (*Foglia v Novello (No 2)* [1981]).

The case has been criticised on the grounds that the Court of Justice had entered into a review of the national court's decision to refer. The purpose of Art 267 TFEU (formerly Art 234 TEC) is that there should be co-operation between national courts and the Court of Justice. If the Court of Justice is to enter into inquiries as to whether the national court's decision to refer is a correct decision, then it is exercising some sort of appellate jurisdiction. It had always been keen to emphasise that it performs an equal but different role in relation to Art 267 TFEU (formerly Art 234 TEC) proceedings, but in the *Foglia* cases it suggested, by reviewing decisions of national courts, that it is higher in a hierarchy to national courts.

▶ FOGLIA v NOVELLO (Case 104/79)

The parties to the action had inserted a clause in their contract in order to induce the Italian court to seek a ruling that the French tax system for liqueur wines was invalid. The Court of Justice declined to give a ruling.

In the 1990s, the CJ began to invoke the principle set out in *Foglia* again in order to control admissibility over preliminary rulings emanating from the national courts of the Member States. Craig and de Búrca have identified four categories of cases in which the Court may decline jurisdiction.

▪ Where the question referred is hypothetical in nature: *Criminal Proceedings against Gasparini and others* [2006];

▪ Where answers to the questions referred would not resolve the dispute before the national court: *Meilicke* [1992]; *Corsica Ferries Italia Srl v Corpo dei Piloti del Porto di Genova* [1994]; *Monin* [1994]; *Dias* [1992];

▪ Where the questions referred do not allow the Court of Justice to see why an answer is necessary: *Barcardi-Martini SAS and Cellier des Dauphins v Newcastle United Football Club* [2003].

In this case, the Court refused to respond to a requested reference. The case concerned a dispute between the claimant drinks manufacturers and the defendant football club. The claimant alleged that the club had pressurised a third party, Dorna Marketing Ltd, to withdraw adverts for the claimant's products from perimeter advertising hoardings during a UEFA cup match between Newcastle United and Metz, of France. Newcastle had taken this action because the game was to be televised in France but French law prohibits the advertising of alcohol on television.

The claimant's High Court action alleged that the club had induced Dorna to break its contract with the claimants. The judge referred the case to the Court of Justice, seeking guidance on the compatibility of the French law with Community law regarding freedom to provide services (Art 56 TFEU (formerly Art 49 EC Treaty)). However, the requested reference was declared inadmissible. The Court stated:

> ... it is essential for national courts to explain ... why they consider that a reply to their questions is necessary to enable them to give judgment ... the Court must display special vigilance when ... a question is referred to it with a view to permitting the national court to decide whether the legislation of another Member State is in accordance with Community law.

■ Where the facts are not set out clearly enough for the Court of Justice to apply the relevant law: *Telemarsicabruzzo* [1993].

INTERPRETATION AND APPLICATION

There is a division of competence between the Court of Justice and the national courts. The CJ's role is to give an authoritative ruling as to the interpretation or validity of the Treaty provision or EU act, while the national courts apply the ruling to the facts of the case. In other words, the ECJ's role is to interpret, while the national court's role is to apply. In *Costa v ENEL* [1964], the Court of Justice said:

> ... [Art 267 TFEU (formerly Art 234 TEC)] gives the court no jurisdiction either to apply the Treaty to a specific case or to decide upon the validity of a provision of domestic law in relation to the Treaty, as it would be possible for it to do under [Art 258 TFEU (formerly Art 226 TEC)].

The distinction between interpretation and application can be very difficult to make. In addition, an abstract interpretation may not be of assistance to the national court. In the *LTM* case [1966], the national court had informed the CJ of the facts of the case. When one of the applicants argued that the question was one of application, the CJ replied:

> Although the Court has no jurisdiction to take cognisance of the application of the Treaty to a specific case, it may extract from the elements of the case those questions of interpretation and validity which alone fall within its jurisdiction.

EFFECT OF A PRELIMINARY REFERENCE

A judgement given by the Court on a preliminary reference is binding on the national court which referred the question for consideration (*Milch-Fett und Eierkontor* [1969]).

The Arsenal case

However, in *Arsenal FC v Reed* [2002], the English High Court made a landmark decision when it refused to apply a preliminary ruling that the High Court itself had requested. Arsenal objected to the activities of the defendant, whom it accused of selling unofficial memorabilia, principally scarves, bearing trade mark protected words ('Arsenal' and 'Gunners') and symbols (a cannon and shield) without permission. It accused him of breaching its trade marks. The defendant contended that his customers understood that his goods were not official Arsenal memorabilia but were regarded simply as 'badges of support, loyalty or affiliation'. He pointed out that he also sold 'official' Arsenal memorabilia and that notices at his stalls clearly indicated which items were official and which were not. The High Court judge, Laddie J, found as a matter of fact that Reed's unofficial goods 'would not be perceived as indicating' any trade origin (meaning a connection in the course of trade between the goods and the trade mark proprietor) with Arsenal FC. However, he decided to seek a ruling from the Court of Justice concerning the interpretation of the relevant Community legislation, Directive 89/104. The question was whether someone like Reed had a defence to alleged trade mark infringement if his use of the trade marked words and symbols did 'not indicate trade origin'.

The Court of Justice held that 'the essential function of a trade mark is to guarantee the identity of origin of the marked goods to the consumer ... by enabling him, without any possibility of confusion, to distinguish the goods from others which have another origin'. (This suggested that there was no breach, given the High Court's findings that customers would not confuse Reed's unofficial goods with Arsenal's official goods.) However, the CJ went on to make certain findings of fact. It stated that there was 'a clear possibility in the present case' that some of Reed's consumers may interpret the word 'Arsenal' as designating that the goods were official merchandise.

Back in the High Court, Laddie J agreed with Reed that the CJ had overstepped its jurisdiction in making findings of fact. He therefore applied the Court's reasoning as to the 'function' of a trade mark, but did so in order to achieve the opposite conclusion, that is, that there was no breach of trade mark on the facts.

The Court of Appeal subsequently allowed an appeal brought by Arsenal against Laddie J's ruling, reversed his decision and applied the CJ's preliminary ruling. The Court of Appeal was satisfied that the Court of Justice had stayed within its jurisdiction and that Laddie J had misinterpreted the CJ's ruling. Nevertheless, the case serves to remind all concerned of the need for the national courts and the Court of Justice to maintain their respective jurisdictions (CJ deals with interpretation of EU law; national courts decide questions of fact and apply law (as interpreted by the CJ) to those facts).

Preliminary rulings as precedents
Preliminary rulings may also be cited as precedents in common law jurisdictions (*WH Smith, Do-It-All and Payless DIY Ltd v Peterborough CC* [1990]).

Is a preliminary ruling binding in subsequent cases? If the same issue arises again in a later case, then, under the doctrine of *acte clair*, there is no need to make a further reference. However, if the national court is unhappy with the previous ruling, it can make an additional reference, even if the matter is *acte clair* (*Da Costa* [1963]); *CILFIT* [1982]. Indeed, a national court is obliged to either follow the ruling or make a new reference. This position is reflected in s 3(1) of the European Communities Act 1972.

Temporal effects of preliminary rulings
The Court of Justice is of the view that an interpretation given in a preliminary ruling applies from the date the provision entered into force and not simply from the date of the ruling: *Amministrazione delle Finanze dello Stato v*

Denkavit Italiana [1980]; *Amministrazione delle Finanze v Salumi* [1980]; *Amministrazione delle Finanze dello Stato v Ariete* [1980]; *Barra* [1988].

In exceptional circumstances, the Court of Justice has departed from this general rule of retroactivity and declared that the temporal effect of the preliminary ruling on the interpretation of a EU provision is binding on existing legal relationships in the future only except where a similar claim has been brought before a national court before the date of the ruling.

In *Defrenne (No. 2)* [1976], the CJ declared for the first time that Art 157 TFEU (formerly Art 141 TEC) on equal pay between men and women for equal work of equal value had horizontal direct effect in relation to direct and overt discrimination. The CJ limited the temporal effect of its preliminary ruling and held that the judgment could only be relied upon in the case before it and in those cases where legal proceedings had been initiated prior to the ruling being delivered. The CJ was influenced by the serious financial implications claims for backdated pay would have had for private sector employees, which may even have resulted in bankruptcy or insolvency. The CJ was also influenced by the fact that the Commission had not initiated an Art 258 TFEU (formerly Art 226 TEC) action against any of the Member States for failing to secure equal pay for men and women. See also *Barber* [1990].

The CJ may also limit the temporal effect of a preliminary ruling on the validity of a EU measure: *Pinna* [1986].

REFORM

According to Rasmussen (2000) 37 CML Rev 1071, 'It is . . . a generally shared view today that the case for a comprehensive and profound judicial reform has become compelling.' Similarly, Johnston (2001) 38 CML Rev 499 states, 'Clearly, there is a serious workload problem for the Courts, due to a number of factors. . . . it is particularly serious in the context of references for a preliminary ruling . . .'.

There are several reasons for the 'workload problem':

- The increasing number of Member States means more courts and tribunals, which means more referrals. In 2005 the Court of Justice gave rulings in 254 cases. In 2008 it delivered 301 preliminary rulings. In 2009 the number decreased to 259 delivered preliminary rulings by the court.

- The increasing number of languages: in 2006 there were 27 States with 22 different languages. This has implications for *acte clair*, as well as increasing the burden on the Court's translators.

- The increasing scope and volume of EU legislation.

A solution was adopted in the Treaty of Nice (and has slightly changed with the Lisbon Treaty 2009), which came into effect in February 2003. For the first time, the General Court (formerly CFI) is allowed to deal with some requests for preliminary references. Art 256(3) TFEU (formerly Article 225(3) TEC) provides that the 'General Court' shall have jurisdiction to give preliminary references 'in specific areas' to be laid down by the Statute.

Article 256 TFEU (formerly Article 225 TEC) goes on to provide:

> Where the General Court considers that the case requires a decision of principle likely to affect the unity or consistency of Union law, it may refer the case to the Court of Justice for a ruling.

> Decisions given by the General Court on questions referred for a preliminary ruling may exceptionally be subject to review by the Court of Justice, under the conditions and within the limits laid down by the Statute, where there is a serious risk of the unity or consistency of Union law being affected.

There are potential problems with this provision:

Interpretation. What does 'specific areas' involve? Other ambiguous words or phrases include 'decision of principle', 'likely to affect the unity or consistency', 'exceptionally', and 'serious risk'.

Procedure. Under this procedure, when would the General Court (formerly CFI) be able to refer the case on? At the start of the case, or at any time? Some guidance may be sought from the procedure of the European Court of Human Rights (ECtHR).

OTHER REFORM PROPOSALS

Note some other reforms that have been suggested in recent years. Arguments for and against are given below.

Restrict the right to seek references to national 'courts-of-last-resort' only

(For example the House of Lords.) This was proposed by the Court of Justice and the General Court themselves in a consultation paper (1999). It was rejected by a special working group organised by the European Commission in 2000.

For: this would reduce the CJ's workload by approximately 75 per cent.

Against: it threatens uniformity of EU law; threatens the dialogue that presently exists between CJ and national courts; and would transfer problems to national systems, as parties would seek to keep appealing until they reached the court-of-last-resort.

Abolish the right of first-instance national courts and tribunals to seek references

This would affect county courts, magistrates' courts and most tribunals. The House of Lords, Court of Appeal, High Court (at least when acting as an appeal court), and certain tribunals (such as the Employment Appeal Tribunal and Immigration Appeal Tribunal) would all retain power to request references.

For: the CJ's workload would be reduced by approximately 25 per cent.

Against: it threatens the uniformity of EU law; it could transfer problems to national systems, as parties would seek to appeal at least once.

'Case filtering'

The idea is that the CJ should be allowed to select cases according to their novelty, complexity or importance.

For: this would obviously lead to a reduced CJ workload; it might prompt national courts to be more selective; it would allow the CJ to concentrate on those cases which are 'fundamental' to the uniformity and development of EU law.

Against: it threatens the uniformity of EU law; it could distort the judicial dialogue between the CJ and national courts – the latter may not risk seeking a reference being rebuffed and, therefore, not send it.

Reword Art 267 TFEU (formerly Art 234 TEC)

In 1999 the European Commission proposed adding a sentence to the end of what is presently the second paragraph of the Article, requiring national courts to 'specify why the validity or interpretation of the rule of Union law raises difficulties in the case before it'. It was also proposed that the second and third paragraphs should be amended to impose a precondition that the question 'is of sufficient importance to Union law and that there is reasonable doubt as to the answer to that question'.

'Decentralisation'

This is perhaps the most radical reform, proposed by Jacques and Weiler (1990) 27 CML Rev 185, involving creating a series of regional courts to handle preliminary references. The Court of Justice would be installed at 'the apex of the system' and would be renamed 'European High Court of Justice' (EHCJ). National 'supreme' court references would go directly to the EHCJ. Below it would be four new 'Community Regional Courts' (CRCs) with 'jurisdiction to receive preliminary references from, and issue preliminary rulings to, national courts within each region'. They added, 'The legal status of the decision and rulings is a delicate matter'. They envisaged a hierarchical system with the EHCJ binding the CRCs. CRCs would be 'respectful' of each other but 'need not consider themselves strictly bound'.

For: a dramatically reduced workload for the CJ; the CRCs could develop specialist expertise.

Against: there would be a risk of divergent rulings from the various CRCs.

Innovations with the Lisbon Treaty

With the disappearance of the pillar structure the jurisdiction of the Court of Justice extends to the law of the EU, save where provided otherwise in the Treaties. It has thus acquired general jurisdiction to give preliminary rulings in the area of freedom, security and justice following the repeal of former Arts 35 EU and 68 EC, which imposed restrictions on its jurisdiction. With regard to police and judicial co-operation in criminal matters the jurisdiction of the Court to give preliminary rulings is binding and will no longer be subject to a declaration by each Member State recognising that jurisdiction and specifying the national courts that may request a preliminary ruling (see transitional provisions for limitations).

As regards visas, asylum, immigration and other policies related to free movement of persons *any* national court or tribunal (not just the higher courts) will now be able to request preliminary rulings.

The preliminary ruling procedure has been extended to acts of the EU bodies, offices or agencies (Art 267 TFEU) This new rule also provides that the Court of Justice is required to act with the minimum of delay if a question referred for a preliminary ruling is raised in a case pending before any court of tribunal of a Member State with regard to a person in custody.

You should now be confident that you would be able to tick all of the boxes on the checklist at the beginning of this chapter. To check your knowledge of Preliminary rulings why not visit the companion website and take the Multiple Choice Question test. Check your understanding of the terms and vocabulary used in this chapter with the flashcard glossary.

5

Free movement of persons and citizenship

Explain the scope of Article 45 TFEU (formerly Article 39 TEC) ☐

Identify the different categories of persons that can benefit from the right to free movement of persons ☐

Discuss what is meant by an EU worker with reference to the case law ☐

Explain the concept of Union citizenship and identify the rights of a European citizen ☐

Discuss the significance and key features of Directive 2004/38 ☐

Explain how a Member State can limit the rights of free movement of persons on grounds of public policy, public security and public health ☐

INTRODUCTION

FREE MOVEMENT OF PERSONS

Workers

Article 45 TFEU (formerly Article 39 of the *EC Treaty*) provides for free movement of workers. Secondary legislation provides for detailed rules governing the right of entry into the territory of a Member State to carry out an economic activity, the right to remain in a Member State after having been employed there, and the right to equality of access to and conditions of employment on the same basis as nationals of the host State. These rights are subject to exceptions contained in the Treaty concerning public policy, public security and public health, and an exemption in the case of public service. Limited rights have also been conferred on job-seekers.

Self-employed

Article 49 TFEU (formerly Art 43 TEC) provides for the free movement of the self-employed. It prohibits restrictions on the freedom of establishment of nationals of Member States in the territory of another Member State and provides that freedom establishment includes the right to take up and pursue activities as self-employed.

It confers the right to take up and pursue activities, as well as set up and manage a business. Article 56 TFEU (formerly Art 49 TEC) provides for the free movement of those providing or receiving a service (free movement of services). Both sets of provisions are subject to exceptions contained in the Treaties concerning public policy, public security and public health (Art 52 TFEU (formerly Art 46 TEC) and Art 62 TFEU (formerly Art 55 EC)) an exemption in the case of activities connected with the exercise of 'official authority' (Art 51 TFEU (formerly Art 45 TEC) and Art 62 TFEU (formerly Art 55 TEC)).

Family members

Secondary legislation also confers rights on family members in recognition of the fact that workers and the self-employed are unlikely to exercise their right to free movement if they are unable to take their family with them to the host State.

Articles 45, 49 and 56 TFEU (formerly Arts 39, 43 and 49 TEC) are said to represent an application of the fundamental principle of non-discrimination contained in Art 18 TFEU (formerly Art 12 TEC) in the context of free movement of persons and services. The Court of Justice has also ruled that non-discriminatory measures may be caught by Art 45 (*Bosman* [1995]), Art 49 (*Gebhard* [1995]) and 56 TFEU (*Alpine Investments* [1995]) unless they can be objectively justified and are proportionate.

Non-economically active

Initially, the right of free movement without discrimination was given to 'economically active' persons and their families, the purpose being to allow economically active persons the freedom to move around the Union so that 'workers' and the self-employed could move to jobs and higher wages in other parts of the Union.

In 1990, freedom of movement was extended to three categories of persons who were not economically active – students, retired persons and persons of independent means.

CITIZENSHIP

The Treaty on European Union establishes European citizenship, so that every person holding the nationality of a Member State is to be a citizen of the Union: Art 20 TFEU (formerly Art 17 TEC). Nationality is conferred by the national law of the State concerned. In the UK, the relevant legislation is the British Nationality Act 1981 (as amended by the British Overseas Territories Act 2002): *Kaur* [2001].

Article 21 TFEU (formerly Article 18 TEC) confirms the right of free movement of all EU citizens. Art 21(1) TFEU states that:

> 'Every citizen of the Union will have the right to move and reside freely within the territory of the Member States, subject to the limitations and conditions laid down in the Treaties and by measures adopted to give them effect.'

Articles 22–24 TFEU (formerly Articles 19–21 TEC) confers new political rights on EU citizens. Art 22 TFEU (formerly Art 19 TEC) confers on EU citizens residing in a Member State of which he/she is not a national the right to vote and to stand as a candidate at local elections and elections to the European Parliament under the same conditions as nationals. Art 23 TFEU (formerly Art 20 TEC) provides that every EU citizen enjoy diplomatic or consular protection of any of the Member States when in the territory of a third country under the same conditions as nationals. Art 24 TFEU (formerly Art 21 TEC) grants EU citizens the right to petition the European Parliament, the right to apply to the Ombudsman and the right to write to any of the Union institutions or bodies in one of the official languages of the EU and to receive a reply in the same language. Arts 227 and 228 TFEU (formerly Arts 194 and 195 TEC) extend the first two rights to 'any natural or legal person established in the Union' which includes non-EU nationals resident in the EU.

Article 21 (1) TFEU (formerly Art 18(1) TEC) would seem to confer the right of free movement on all citizens and not simply those covered by the original Treaty provisions and secondary legislation (discussed below). However, initially this was not the case. In a 1993 report issued by the European Commission shortly after the TEU, it stated that it was not necessary to introduce new secondary legislation to give effect to Art 21 TFEU (formerly Art 18 TEC). Thus, Union citizenship was initially thought to be of symbolic significance only and the right to free movement and residence was to be restricted to those granted under Arts 45, 49 and 56 TFEU (formerly Arts 39, 43 and 49 TEC) and the accompanying secondary legislation.

However, the Court of Justice adopted a different view and has given the concept of Union citizenship set out in Art 21 TFEU (formerly Art 18 TEC) an independent meaning in relation to EU citizens who are lawfully resident in other Member States.

▶ BAUMBAST (Case C-413/99)

The Court of Justice has recognised that Art 21 TFEU (formerly Article 18 TEC) has direct effect. In *Baumbast* [2002], the Court held that, 'As regards, in particular, the right to reside within the territory of the Member States under Art 18 (now 21 TFEU), that right is conferred directly on every citizen of the Union by a clear and precise provision of the EC Treaty.' The Court did go on to qualify this statement in the next paragraph, where it emphasised that, 'Admittedly, that right for citizens of the Union to reside within the territory of another Member State is conferred subject to the limitations and conditions laid down by the EC Treaty and by the measures adopted to give it effect.'

The concept of Union citizenship has been drawn upon by the Court of Justice in conjunction with Art 18 TFEU (formerly Art 12 TEC) to grant EU citizens lawfully resident in another Member State equal treatment in access to various social benefits. The CJ has emphasised that any limitations or conditions on the right to equal treatment must be applied in accordance with the principle of proportionality. This case law has had an important impact on the existing legal framework relating to free movement of persons. However, it is important to read the citizenship case law in conjunction with the existing provisions on free movement of persons. It does mean that in practice there are different rights for different categories of persons. Greater rights are conferred on the economically active than the non-economically active.

The developments in the case law led to the enactment of Directive 2004/38, which came into force on 30 April 2006. It consolidates into a single directive most of the EU secondary legislation and some of the case law concerning the right of entry and residence of all previous categories of persons (workers, self-employed, family members, job-seekers, students, retired persons, persons of independent means), under the single category of 'citizens'. The previously essential link between migration and being economically active has been removed. Barnard has explained that, 'At the heart of the directive lies the basic idea that the rights enjoyed by the migrant citizen and their family members increase the longer a person is resident': Barnard, C., *The Substantive Law of the EU*, 2nd edition, Oxford: OUP, 2007.

Pre–2006 Secondary Legislation	Post-2006 Secondary Legislation
Dir 64/221 – Right of Member States to derogate from the free movement provisions on grounds of public policy, security and health (Derogation Directive)	Replaced by Dir 2004/38
Dir 68/360 – Rights of Entry and Residence of Workers, Self-Employed and Family Members	Replaced by Dir 2004/38
Reg 1612/68 – Right to Equal Treatment of Workers and Family Members	Amended by Dir 2004/38 and Regulations 312/76 and 2434/82
Reg 1251/70 – Right to Remain in a Member State after having been employed there.	Replaced by Dir 2004/38
Dir 90/365 – Rights of Retired Persons and their families	Replaced by Dir 2004/38

Pre–2006 Secondary Legislation	Post–2006 Secondary Legislation
Dir 90/366 as amended by Dir 93/96 – Rights of Students and their Families	Replaced by Dir 2004/38
Dir 90/364 – Rights of Persons of Independent Means and their Families	Replaced by Dir 2004/38
Dir 73/148 – Rights of Entry and Residence	Replaced by Dir 2004/38 with regard to freedom of establishment (self-employed) only
Dir 75/34 – Rights of the Self-Employed to Remain	Replaced by Dir 2004/38 Directive 2008/104/EC Directive 2008/94/EC

Note that most of Regulation 1612/68 is still in force. Only Arts 10 and 11 have been repealed and up-dated and replaced by Arts 2 and 3 of Directive 2004/38. The Directive has been transposed into UK law by the Immigration (European Economic Area) Regulations 2006.

Treaty of Amsterdam and the Schengen Agreement

The Treaty of Amsterdam inserted a new title into the former EC Treaty called 'visa, asylum, immigration and the free movement of persons'. This moves much of the old third pillar of the European Union into the EC Treaty itself. It also incorporates the Schengen Agreement and the Schengen Implementing Convention into EC law. The changes brought about by the Schengen Agreement include the abolition of border controls between participating States. The UK, Ireland and Denmark have opted out of most of the provisions of the Schengen Agreement.

2004 Enlargement

Prior to enlargement on 1 May 2004 and 1 January 2007, Member States of the European Union expressed their fear of a massive arrival of workers from the new Member States. In response to these concerns, there are transitional arrangements regarding the sensitive issue of free movement of workers within the enlarged Union. The 15 Member States could allow total or partial freedom of movement for workers from the new Member States during this transitional period, which may last up to a maximum of seven years from the date of accession. The following notes relate to free movement of workers as it applies to the 15 Member States (i.e. not to those states which **may** be subject to the transitional arrangements).

DEFINITION OF A 'WORKER'

The term 'worker' is not defined in the Treaty or any of the relevant secondary legislation. It is an EU concept and is not derived from national law. EU legislation and case law make it clear that a 'worker' is an employed person, irrespective of whether he performs managerial or manual functions.

The CJ has given a wide definition to the term 'worker'. In *Levin* [1982], a chambermaid, whose part time earnings fell below the Dutch minimum wage, supplemented these earnings with her own private income and had only taken the job to obtain the right to reside in the Netherlands. She was held to come within the EU definition of 'worker'.

> ▶ LEVIN [1982]
>
> **Mrs Levin was a British national working in Holland as a chambermaid for 20 hours per week. She was financially supported by her South African husband.**
>
> The CJ held that she was a worker even though she had taken the job simply to qualify for worker status.

The applicant in *Levin* had not been a charge on the State and had supplemented her low level of earnings by her own private means. However, a person is still classified as a 'worker' if their earnings need to be augmented by supplementary benefit. In *Kempf* [1987], a German resident in the Netherlands who had to have his part time earnings boosted by supplementary benefit was still a 'worker'.

> ▶ KEMPF [1987]
>
> A German music teacher who gave twelve lessons a week in the Netherlands was regarded as a worker for the purposes of Art 45 TFEU (formerly Art 39 EC Treaty).

FREE MOVEMENT OF PERSONS AND CITIZENSHIP

The definition of 'worker' has been extended to trainees (*Lawrie Blum* [1987]), where the applicant was a salaried trainee teacher who initially performed her duties under supervision but later independently came within the definition of 'worker'.

The CJ said that the test for a *Community* 'worker' was whether someone was in genuine and effective employment and performing services for an employer under his direction and control in return for remuneration.

In *Bernini* [1992], the CJ said that in determining whether a trainee was in 'genuine and effective' employment, the national court may require proof that the trainee had worked long enough to become fully acquainted with the job performed.

The meaning of 'genuine and effective employment' was further considered in *Steymann* [1988]. A German national joined a Bhagwan community in the Netherlands. He was a qualified plumber and performed plumbing tasks for the community, and also carried out general domestic tasks and assisted in their commercial activities. He was not given formal wages but was given board, lodging and pocket money.

The CJ considered whether the work was genuine and effective, and it was held that he was a worker even though he did not receive any direct remuneration. The benefits which the Community gave to its members were considered to be an indirect advantage for the work that was performed.

The employment must be a 'real' job. In *Bettray* [1989], Dutch legislation created 'social employment'. Jobs were specially created for people in order to support them, rehabilitate them or increase their capacity for normal work. This was done through State financed work associations, specially created for the purpose. Bettray was a German national living in Holland and was given 'social employment' as part of his treatment for drug addiction. He was receiving remuneration, but was not a 'worker', as the activities could not be regarded as genuine and effective. The job had been created to fit the applicant's capacity for work, as opposed to him being selected to do a particular job.

The CJ continues to give judgments on the scope of the word 'worker', and maintains a flexible approach. In *Ninni-Orasche* [2003], the CJ explicitly held that, although Ms Ninni-Orasche, an Italian national, had only worked for two and a half months (as a waitress) during a period of several years in Austria, she was not excluded from the scope of Article 45 TFEU (formerly Article 39 TEC). The Court declined to impose any minimum thresholds in terms of time worked or money earned. Ultimately, whether or not she was a 'worker' was a question of fact for the national court, applying the 'genuine and effective' test. More recently, in *Trojani* [2004], the Court dealt with a case very similar to *Steymann*. This case involved a French national living in a Salvation Army hostel in Belgium, where he did various odd jobs for 'about 30 hours a week', in return for board and lodging and 'some pocket money', as part of a 'personal socio-occupational re-integration programme'. The Court refused to hold that, as a matter of law, *Trojani* did not satisfy the status of worker leaving this assessment to the national court. Instead the Court offered the following summary of its case law to date:

> Neither the *sui generis* nature of the employment relationship under national law, nor the level of productivity of the person concerned, the origin of the funds from which the remuneration is paid or the limited amount of the remuneration can have any consequence in regard to whether or not the person is a worker for the purposes of Community law.

SELF-EMPLOYED

Self-employed persons do not fall within the scope of the term 'worker'. However, this does not mean that they are unprotected by EU law. Instead, the self-employed fall either under the scope of Art 49 TFEU (formerly Art 43 TEC) (which deals with the right of establishment) or Art 56 TFEU (formerly Art 49 TEC) (the provision and receipt of services). Both Art 49 TFEU (*Reyners* [1974]) and Art 56 TFEU (*Van Binsbergen* [1974]) have direct effect.

In *Allonby v Accrington and Rossendale College* [2004] the CJ widended the meaning of 'workers' to include 'self-employed' persons under the meaning of Art 157(1) TFEU if his independence is merely notional, thereby disguising an employment relationship within the meaning of that article.

Under Art 49 TFEU (formerly Art 43 TEC), self-employed persons are allowed to travel to, reside in and set up a business in another EU Member State without discrimination and without encountering unnecessary obstacles (see below). The CJ has defined the self-employed as someone who 'participates, on a stable and continuous basis, in the economic life of a Member State other than his state of origin and to profit therefrom. . .' . In contrast to a worker, a self-employed person carries out work of economic value for remuneration, but does not pursue an activity under the direction of another or receive a salary. A good example is *Steinhauser* [1985], in which a self-employed German artist used Art 49 TFEU (formerly Art 43 TEC) to establish the right to establish a business selling paintings in the French seaside resort of Biarritz under the same conditions as French nationals.

Under Art 56 TFEU (formerly Art 49 TEC), self-employed persons have the right to travel to other Member States on a temporary or periodic basis to provide services. The temporary nature of the activity being pursued is determined by reference to its duration and 'regularity, periodicity or continuity': *Gebhard* [1995]. A good example is *Van Binsbergen* [1974], where a Dutch law requiring all lawyers who wished to appear in Dutch courts to be habitually resident in the Netherlands was held to be capable of breaching Art 56 TFEU (formerly Art 49 TEC) as it restricted the freedom of lawyers resident in (say) Belgium from offering their legal services in the Netherlands.

Although Art 56 TFEU (formerly Art 49 TEC) refers to the freedom to *provide* services, this provision has been subsequently extended by the CJ to include the freedom to *receive* services: *Luisi v Ministero del Tesoro* [1985]; *Cowan v Le Trésor Public* [1989]. Providers and receivers of services are entitled to the same rights as workers in so far as they are necessary in order to provide/ receive the service.

Self-employed workers in the EU and their partners will enjoy better social protection, including the right to maternity leave for the first time, under new legislation endorsed by EU governments adopted on 24 June 2010. The Directive on self-employed workers and assisting spouses repeals and replaces an earlier law (Directive 86/613/EEC) and improves the social protection rights of millions of women in the labour market. At EU level, this is the first time a maternity allowance has been granted to self-employed workers. The Council of Ministers has formally adopted the legislation on 24 June 2010 without debate following a second reading in the European Parliament. EU countries will have two years to introduce it into national law.

As far as employees are concerned, the EU recently adopted a new Directive improving the right to parental leave (IP/09/1854) and the Commission's proposal for a revised Directive on maternity leave is currently in first reading by the European Parliament (see also IP/08/1450).

FAMILY MEMBERS

It has long been recognised that the family members of the economically active may accompany the worker and self-employed to the host State.

Article 2 of Dir 2004/38 extended the category of family member. A 'family member' can now be defined as follows:

- The spouse of the worker or self-employed person.

- The partner with whom the Union citizen has contracted a registered partnership.

- The direct descendants of the worker or self-employed person who are under the age of 21 or who are dependants and those of the spouse or registered partner.

- The dependent direct relatives in the ascending line and those of the spouse or registered partner.

Under Art 7 of the Directive, family members may accompany or join the worker or self-employed person in the host state (i.e. they have the right of entry).

In addition, Art 3 of the Directive states that the host Member State shall facilitate entry for other persons, namely:

- Any other family members, irrespective of their nationality, who in the country from which they have come, are dependants or members of the household of the Union citizen having the primary right of residence (e.g. the worker) or where serious health grounds strictly require the personal care of the family member by the Union citizen.
- The partner with whom he/she has a stable and duly attested relationship.

The Member state will have to justify any denial of right of entry to the above.

In *Carpenter* [2002], the CJ held that a service provider could be accompanied by his spouse, who was a non-EU national, where a significant proportion of the services were provided in other Member States and where the spouse contributes to the provision of the service by, for example, caring for the service provider's children whilst he is on business trips.

Cohabitees

It can be seen from the above that a cohabitee of the worker or self-employed person will now have their entry to the host state facilitated. Compare the case of *Netherlands v Reed* [1986] argued under the old law.

Separated and divorced spouses

In *Diatta* [1985], the CJ ruled that a separated spouse had the right to reside in the host Member State.

The situation could change if the parties actually divorced.

Directive 2004/38 deals with the question of right of residence for family members in the event of divorce, annulment of marriage or termination of a registered partnership.

In the case of EU family members, those events will not affect the family member's right of residence (Art 13(1)) but in the case of non-EU family members, retention of the right of residence is restricted (e.g. there will be no loss of the right of residence if, prior to divorce, the marriage had lasted at least three years, including one year in the host Member State).

Marriages of convenience

An important limitation was placed on the scope of the word 'spouse' in *Akrich* [2003]. The CJ pointed out that only genuine marriages would be accepted. The Court stated that 'there would be an abuse if the facilities afforded by EU law in favour of migrant workers and their spouses were invoked in the context of marriages of convenience entered into in order to circumvent the provisions relating to entry and residence of nationals of non-Member States'.

Article 35 of Directive 2004/38 now specifically provides that Member States may adopt the necessary measures to refuse, terminate or withdraw any right conferred in the case of abuse of rights or fraud, such as marriages of convenience.

Children of workers

Children of workers are entitled not only to education but also to those rights which facilitate education, for example, rights to grants (*Casagrande* [1974]).

In *Echternach and Moritz* [1990], it was held that where a child returns to his State of origin with his parents after living and studying in another Member State, he may still be entitled to return to the host State without his parents and rely on Art 12, Regulation 1612/68 there, if educational institutions in his State of origin refuse to recognise qualifications obtained in the host State.

In *di Leo* [1990], the child of a migrant worker resident in Germany sought to return to her State of origin to undertake vocational training. There was a nationality requirement under German legislation for the award of financial assistance in respect of courses undertaken abroad.

The CJ held that this nationality requirement was contrary to Art 12, Regulation 1612/68. Effective integration would be impeded if a migrant's family could not choose a course on the same basis as nationals of the host State.

Assistance under Art 12, Regulation 1612/68 is available even if the 'child' is 21 or over and is no longer financially dependent on his parents (*Gaal* [1995]).

THE WHOLLY INTERNAL RULE

In general, a national of a Member State who has never exercised the right of freedom of movement within the EU is unable to rely on Arts 21, 45, 49 or 56 TFEU (formerly Arts 18, 39, 43 or 49 TEC) in purely internal situations.

The leading case with regard to Art 45 TFEU (formerly Art 39 TEC) is *R v Saunders* [1979], involving a woman from Northern Ireland who was convicted of theft at Bristol Crown Court and bound over on condition that she returned to Northern Ireland and did not return to England or Wales for three years. However, within six months she was arrested in Wales. She claimed that this breached Art 45 TFEU (formerly Art 39 TEC), but the Court of Justice disagreed. All the facts were 'internal' to the UK, so EU law did not apply.

However, there is an important exception to this rule under Art 49 TFEU (formerly Art 43 TEC): returnees. People who have left one Member State to obtain qualifications in another Member State have relied on Art 49 TFEU against their home Member State to have these qualifications recognised on their return, allowing them to practise a profession: *Knoors* [1979]; *Bouchoucha* [1990]; *Kraus* [1993]; *Fernández de Bobadilla* [1999]. Many situations may now be covered by Directive 2005/36 on the mutual recognition of professional qualifications.

The Court has followed the same approach with regard to Art 21 TFEU (formerly Art 18 TEC). It held that Art 21 TFEU covers measures which may discourage a national from leaving or returning to their home Member State: *Pusa* [2004]; *Rüffler* [2009]. In *Turpeinen* [2006], T, a Finnish national left Finland and retired to Spain. She received a retirement pension from her former employer taxable only in Finland and in accordance with an agreement between Finland and Spain to prevent double taxation. In 2002, T was informed that she would be subject to a special tax regime which applied to Finnish nationals who had not been domiciled in Finland for three years consecutively. Any income received from Finland was subject to a withholding tax of 35 per cent. T argued that she should be taxed under the general (progressive) tax regime as if she were still domiciled in Finland. The ECJ agreed and held that Art 21 TFEU (formerly Art 18 TEC) precludes national legislation which taxes the retirement pension of a national now settled in another Member State at rate which exceeds that payable if resident in the home Member State. Where the pension is the main source of income, the tax regime should be exactly the same. The right to equal treatment with nationals in the same situation falling within the scope of Community law contained in Art 21 TFEU (formerly Art 18 TEC) requires the same progressive scale, the same tax allowances and the same declaration procedure to apply.

MATERIAL SCOPE OF RIGHTS

Article 45(3) TFEU (formerly Article 39(3) TEC) provides workers with the right to enter and remain in another Member State for the purpose of employment and also to remain in that Member State after the employment has finished. These rights are in outline and have been supplemented by secondary legislation: Regulation 1612/68 and Directive 2004/38.

Article 49 TFEU (formerly Article 43 TEC) grants the right to enter and reside in another Member State to persons wishing to pursue a self-employed activity or set up and manage undertakings in the same conditions as nationals. Note that although there is no equivalent of Regulation 1612/68 which applies to the self-employed, the Court of Justice has relied directly on former Art 12 TEC (now Art 18 TFEU) to grant the self-employed equal rights with nationals in the host State. The new Dir 2004/38 expressly refers to the self-employed.

It is important to note that Dir 2004/38 is an umbrella provision conferring the right to enter and remain in another Member State without discrimination on all EU citizens.

THE RIGHT TO ENTER

Rights of residence up to three months

Article 6(1) of Dir 2004/38 grants EU citizens unconditional rights of residence for up to three months in another Member State.

Under Art 6(2) non-EU family members enjoy the same rights as the EU citizen who they have accompanied or joined. However, they may be subject to a visa requirement under Regulation 539/2001. This right of residence of three months is subject to Art 14(1) of Directive 2004/38, i.e. 'as long as they do not become an unreasonable burden on the social assistance system of the host Member State'.

Rights of residence for more than three months

After three months, the right of residence is conditional. Article 7(1) of Dir 2004/38 grants EU citizens the right of residence for more than three months in the host State if:

- they are workers or self-employed; or
- they have sufficient resources for themselves and their family so as not to be a burden on the social assistance system of the host Member State and they have comprehensive sickness insurance cover; or
- they are enrolled on a course of study and have sufficient resources for themselves and their family so as not to be a burden on the social assistance system of the host Member State and they have comprehensive sickness insurance cover; or
- they are family members and satisfy the conditions set out above.

Article 7(2) of Dir 2004/38 grants the right of residence for more than three months to non-EU family members provided the conditions relating to sufficient resources and medical insurance set out in Art 7(1) of Dir 2004/38 are satisfied.

Although residence permits are abolished for EU citizens, Art 8 of the directive provides that Member States **may** require EU citizens to register with the competent authorities within a period of not less than three months from the date of arrival. A registration certificate will be issued immediately but in order for this to be issued, Member States may only require a valid identity card or passport and confirmation of engagement from an employer or a certificate of employment in the case of an EU worker.

Article 9 applies to non-EU family members who must apply for a residence card not less than three months from their date of arrival. This card is valid for five years. Art 10(2) sets out the documentation required before a card will be issued.

Rights of permanent residence

Article 16 of Directive 2004/38 indicates the conditions under which EU citizens and their families may enjoy the right of permanent residence. Briefly, this right exists for EU citizens and their families (including non-EU family members) if they have resided lawfully for a continuous period of five years in the host Member State.

Article 16(3) makes provision for temporary absences and Art 16(4) provides that the right of permanent residence may only be lost through absences of more than two consecutive years. Article 17 details the shorter qualifying period of residence for EU citizens and their families where the worker or self-employed person has retired, or become incapacitated or died.

Rights of residence of work seekers

We have seen that all EU citizens have the right of residence for up to three months under Art 6 of Directive 2004/38. After three months, Art 14(4) provides that an expulsion measure cannot be taken against such persons if they entered the host Member State in order to seek employment if they can provide evidence that they are continuing to seek employment and that they have a genuine chance of being engaged.

This provision reflects the previous case law of the CJ which interpreted former Art 39(3) TEC (now Art 45 TFEU) purposively to give job-seekers the right to enter and reside in another State in order to seek work: *Royer* [1976]; *Antonissen* [1991]. The CJ recognised that the free movement of persons would be undermined if nationals could only move to another Member State if they had an offer of employment. It should be noted that recital 9 of the Preamble of Dir 2004/38 states that this provision is 'without prejudice to the more favourable treatment applicable to job-seekers as recognised by the case-law of the Court of Justice'.

> ### ▶ ANTONISSEN [1991]
>
> **The UK authorities sought to deport a Belgian national who had failed to find work after six months.**
>
> The Court of Justice held that whilst a period of six months was reasonable, the right to remain in the host State to seek work continues as long as the job-seeker can prove that he/she is actively seeking work and has a genuine chance of being employed.

ACCESS TO EMPLOYMENT/EQUALITY OF TREATMENT

There is a prohibition against discrimination on grounds of nationality laid down in general terms by Art 18 TFEU (formerly Art 12 of the EC Treaty).

Regulation 1612/68 gives substance to the provisions of Art 18 TFEU (formerly Art 12 TEC) and Art 45 TFEU (formerly Art 39 of the EC Treaty for workers and their families. The Regulation is divided into three titles: Title I covering eligibility for employment, Title II concerning employment and equality of treatment and Title III, which deals with families' rights (Arts 10 and 11 under this title have been repealed by Directive 2004/38). Note that there is no equivalent for self-employed persons who have had to rely directly on Arts 49 and 18 TFEU (formerly Arts 43 and 12 TEC) to secure equal treatment. Regulation 1612/68 has been partially amended by Regulation 312/76 and Regulation 2434/92.

It is important to remember that since the CJ's judgment in *Martínez Sala* [1998] and *Grzelczyk* [2001], social advantages (see below), which were not previously available to job-seekers, students, retired persons and persons of independent means, are now available to all EU citizens lawfully resident in a Member State on the same basis as nationals in accordance with Arts 21 and 18 TFEU (formerly Arts 18 and 12 of the EC Treaty).

Article 24(1) of Dir 2004/38 confers the right of equal treatment to all EU citizens residing in the territory of the host State in matters falling within the scope of the Treaty. This right also applies to non-EU family members who have the right of residence or permanent residence in the host State. Article 24(2) of Dir 2004/38 permits Member States to derogate from Art 24(1) of Dir 2004/38 in certain circumstances. It states that, 'host Member States shall not be obliged to confer entitlement to social assistance during the first three months of residence or, where appropriate, the longer period provided for in Art 14(4)(b) [which applies to job-seekers], nor shall it be obliged, prior to acquisition of the right of permanent residence, to grant maintenance aid for studies, including vocational training, consisting in student grants or student loans to persons other than workers, self-employed persons, persons who retain such status and members of their families'.

There is an evident tension between the Court's progressive citizenship case law and Art 24(2) of Dir 2004/38. It has been suggested by Craig and de Búrca that Art 24(2) of Dir 2004/38 does not prevent non-economically active EU citizens lawfully resident in a Member State from relying on Arts 18 and 21 TFEU (formerly Arts 12 and 18 TEC) to obtain social advantages on an equal basis with nationals. Any limitations imposed by the Member States must be applied in a proportionate manner.

REGULATION 1612/68: Rights of Workers and their family members

Eligibility for employment (Arts 1–6 – Regulation 1612/68)

Any national of a Member State has the right to take up activity as an employed person and pursue such activity in the territory of another Member State, under the same conditions as nationals of that State: Art 1, Regulation 1612/68.

It is not possible to restrict the number or allocate a certain percentage of foreign workers to be employed in an activity or area of activity: Art 4, Regulation 1612/68.

States are entitled to permit the imposition on non-nationals of conditions 'relating to linguistic knowledge required by reason of the nature of the post to be filled': Art 3(1), Regulation 1612/68. In practice, this is one of the most important barriers to free movement. Workers are inhibited from moving to other States, as they do not speak the language. Art 3(1) permits a requirement of linguistic knowledge where that is required for the post.

Language requirements can be imposed where there is an official policy to promote the language: *Groener v Minister for Education* [1989]. Teachers in Irish schools are required to be proficient in the Irish language. Under the Irish Constitution, Irish is the first official language of Ireland and national law had a clear policy of maintaining and promoting the Irish language. In *Groener*, the applicant was a Dutch woman who was barred from appointment as an art teacher at a college of marketing and design because she was unable to obtain the certificate. The Irish Government claimed that their action was justified on the basis of Art 3(1), Regulation 1612/68.

It was held that the TFEU (formerly EC Treaty) does not prohibit the promotion by a Member State of its national language, provided that the measures taken to implement it are not disproportionate to the objective pursued and do not discriminate against the nationals of Member States. As teachers have a role in the promotion of Irish, a requirement that they have knowledge of Irish was reasonable provided it was applied in a non-discriminatory manner and the level of knowledge to be attained must not be excessive in relation to the objective pursued.

Equality of treatment (Arts 7–9 – Regulation 1612/68 as amended by Regulation 312/76)

Article 7(1), Regulation 1612/68 provides that workers must be treated equally in respect of any conditions of employment and work, in particular remuneration, dismissal and, should a worker become unemployed, re-instatement or re-employment.

This covers both direct and indirect discrimination. In *Ugliola* [1969], a German employer took into account, for the purposes of seniority, employees' periods of national service in Germany. The applicant had done his national service in Italy and so it did not count. This was held to be discriminatory.

Social and tax advantages

Under Art 7(2), a migrant worker is entitled to the same 'social and tax advantages' as national workers.

The term 'social advantage' has been interpreted widely. In *Fiorini v SNCF* [1975], it was held to include a special rail reduction card to parents of large families, even though that is a benefit which does not attach to contracts of employment.

> ▶ **FIORINI v SNCF [1975]**
>
> The widow of a deceased Italian migrant worker, who was resident in France, was entitled to a fare reduction granted to families of French workers. The fare reduction was regarded as a social advantage which could not be interpreted restrictively.

A formula was developed for determining 'social or tax advantages' in *Ministère Public v Even* [1979]:

> Social or tax advantages are 'those which, whether or not linked to a contract of employment, are generally granted to national workers primarily because of their objective status as workers or by virtue of the mere fact of their residence on national territory'.

An excellent example of Art 7(2) in practice is *Mutsch* [1985]. M was a German-speaking Luxembourg national resident in Belgium. He got into a fight with police and was subject to criminal proceedings. He claimed the right to have the case conducted in German. Belgian legislation provides that criminal proceedings may be heard in German if the accused so requests – but this right was available only to Belgian nationals. The CJ held that Art 7(2) applied. Thus, the right to have a criminal prosecution conducted in German constituted a 'social and tax advantage'. It is important to note that M had this right only because Belgian nationals had the same right. Had he been working in the UK, for example, he would not have been able to insist on trial in German, because UK nationals have no such right either.

Social and tax advantages do, however, include benefits granted on a discretionary basis (*Reina* [1982]). An Italian couple were living in Germany. The husband was a 'worker' and they applied for a childbirth loan which was State-financed from the defendant bank. The loan was payable under German law to German nationals living in Germany. The bank argued that it was not a 'social advantage' under Art 7(2) as the loan had a political purpose: it was designed to increase the number of Germans. It was also a discretionary loan. It was also argued that the loan would be hard to recover from foreign nationals who returned home. The CJ, applying the *Even* formula, held that the benefit granted on a discretionary basis was a social advantage.

Similarly, in *Castelli* [1984], an Italian, on being widowed, went to live with her son in Belgium. Applying the *Even* formula, it was held that she was entitled to claim a guaranteed income paid to all old people in Belgium. She had a right to reside with her son and so was entitled to the same social and tax advantages as Belgian workers and ex-workers.

> ### ▶ CASTELLI [1984]
>
> The Italian mother residing with her son, a migrant worker in Belgium, was entitled to the same social advantages as a Belgian family member.

It was held in *O'Flynn* [1996] that an allowance such as a funeral payment was within Art 7(2).

In *Baldinger* [2004], the CJ decided that a war allowance paid by the Austrian government to former prisoners-of-war was not a 'social advantage', drawing attention to the fact that it was not 'linked to the status of worker'. This is, at first glance, difficult to reconcile with *Fiorini*, where the Court explicitly held that benefits need not be linked to any 'contract of employment'. Perhaps the answer is that the only possible claimants were Austrian nationals who had been taken as POWs during World War I and/or II, who would, therefore, be in their early 70s *at least*, which is above the normal retirement age.

In *Lebon* [1987], the CJ held that a person who is seeking work, but has never worked, that is, a person in the *Antonissen* situation considered above, can only benefit from the right to equal treatment with regard to access to employment (Arts 2 and 5 of Regulation 1612/68), but is not entitled to claim 'social and tax advantages'. However, this decision was overruled in recent case law, which was interpreted in light of the right to equal treatment embodied in the concept of EU citizenship introduced in 1993 and laid down in Arts 20 and 21 TFEU (formerly Arts 17 and 18 of the EC Treaty). In *Collins* [2004], involving a dual Irish-American national seeking work in the UK who had been turned down for job-seeker's allowance, a social security benefit available to those looking for work in the UK and conditional on a residence requirement, the CJ held that his application should be considered and not automatically rejected:

'In view of the establishment of citizenship of the Union and the interpretation in the case-law of the right to equal treatment enjoyed by citizens of the Union (*Grzelczyk* [2001]), it is no longer possible to exclude from the scope of [Art 45(2) TFEU] (former Article 39(2) EC Treaty) – which expresses the fundamental principle of equal treatment, guaranteed by [Art 18 TFEU] (formerly Article 12 TEC) – a benefit of a financial nature intended to facilitate access to employment in the labour market of a Member State' (para 63).

'The interpretation of the scope of the principle of equal treatment in relation to *access* to employment must reflect this development as compared with the interpretation followed in *Lebon* and in Case C-278/94 *Commission v Belgium*' (para 64).

The *Collins* ruling was confirmed in *Ioannidis* [2005] where it was held to be unlawful for a Greek national to be refused entitlement to a job seeker's allowance for his first employment in Belgium on the grounds that he had received his secondary education outside Belgium.

Vocational training

Article 7(3) entitles workers to access, under the same conditions as national workers, and to training in vocational schools and retraining centres.

The extent to which this provision applied to education was considered by the CJ in *Brown* [1988] and *Lair* [1989]. Brown had obtained a place at Cambridge University to study engineering, and Lair had obtained a place at the University of Hanover to read languages. They claimed grants from the UK and German authorities respectively. Although Brown had dual French/British nationality, he and his family had been domiciled in France for many years. He obtained sponsorship from Ferranti and worked for them in Scotland for eight months, which was intended as a preparation for his university studies. Lair, a French national, had worked intermittently in Germany for five years with spells of involuntary unemployment. The authorities refused to give them grants.

The refusals were challenged under, *inter alia*, Art 7(2) and Art 7(3), Regulation 1612/68.

In both cases, the Court held that neither course constituted 'training in vocational schools' for the purpose of Art 7(3). The parties could succeed only under Art 7(2). The Court held that because Brown had acquired the status of a worker as a result of his acceptance into university, he could not rely upon Art 7(2). In Lair's case, the court drew a distinction purely between involuntary and voluntary unemployment. In the latter case, the applicant could claim a grant for a course only if there was a link between the studies and the previous work activity.

▶ BROWN [1988]

Brown, a French national, obtained employment in Scotland which was described as pre-university industrial training.

The CJ held that a national of another Member State will not be entitled to a grant for studies by virtue of his status as a worker where it is established that he acquired that status exclusively as a result of his being accepted for admission to university to undertake the studies in question.

▶ LAIR [1989]

Ms Lair, a French national living in Germany, was able to secure a grant for a place at Hanover University provided she could show that her course was connected in some way to her previous employment.

Article 7(3)(d) of Directive 2004/38 now specifically provides that a worker shall retain the status of worker if he/she embarks on vocational training. Unless he/she is involuntarily unemployed, the retention of the status of worker shall require the training to be related to the previous employment.

Brown was an attempt to plug a legal loophole whereby a student could acquire the status of 'worker' and could, therefore, claim all the financial benefits that flow from this under Art 7(2), Regulation 1612/68. In doing so, the CJ has created a different category of 'worker' whereby a person can satisfy the definition of a worker under Art 45 TFEU (formerly Art 39 EC) but may not qualify for all the rights which flow from this.

The importance of the ruling in *Brown* has diminished dramatically since the Court's decision in *Grzelczyk* [2001] and *Bidar* [2005], in which the Court drew upon the concept of citizenship set out in Art 21 TFEU (formerly Art 18 TEC), combined with the principle of non-discrimination in Art 18 TFEU (formerly Art 12 TEC), to change its earlier restrictions on the entitlements of students to social welfare and to maintenance grants in the host Member States.

In *Grzelczyk*, G, a French national, was studying physical education at a university in Belgium. For the first three years, he had supported himself through his studies by taking on minor jobs and obtaining credit facilities. At the start of his final year, he applied for financial assistance, the minimex, from the Belgian social service to allow him to concentrate on his dissertation and practical training. This was refused on the basis that the minimex was only payable to Belgian nationals and migrant Community workers. The CJ decided that, as a migrant student, he was lawfully resident in Belgium in accordance with Directive 93/96 on Students' Residence Rights. However, this did not entitle him to the minimex. The CJ held that as an EU citizen lawfully resident in another Member State, he could rely on Art 18 TFEU (formerly Art 12 TEC) in all situations falling within the scope of the Treaty, including the right of free movement set out in Art 21 TFEU (formerly Art 18 TEC). The Court noted several changes since *Brown*, in which assistance given to students for maintenance and training fell outside the scope of the Treaty, such as the introduction of citizenship by the TEU and a new EC Treaty title on education. It acknowledged that Art 21 TFEU (formerly Art 18 TEC) is subject to limitations and conditions and that the Dir 93/96 requires students to have sufficient resources and medical insurance. However, it stated that there was no provision which expressly precludes students from receiving social security benefits. The 'sufficient resources' requirement did not specify a particular amount and simply required a declaration to be made which had to be truthful at the time it was made. The CJ accepted that the student's financial position could change over time for reasons beyond their control. The Court added that a Member State could conclude that an application for social security benefits by a student meant that the 'sufficient resources' requirement was no longer satisfied and could withdraw the right to residence. However, this conclusion could not be the automatic response to an application for benefits. The Court also referred to the Preamble of the residence directives in force at the time and indicated that although a student should not become an 'unreasonable burden' on the State, it may be implied that a student may legitimately become a 'reasonable' burden on the State. It ruled that the legislation 'thus accepts a certain degree of financial solidarity between nationals of a host Member State and nationals of other Member States, particularly if the difficulties which a beneficiary of the right of residence encounters are temporary' (para 44).

In *Bidar* [2005], B, a student of French nationality, had been living in the UK with his grandmother since 1998. His application for a subsidised loan in 2001 to fund his studies at University College London was refused as he did not meet the criteria, namely that he had to have been resident in the UK for the previous three years. Time spent in full-time secondary education did not count. The CJ held that he could claim a right of equal access to a subsidised loan to cover his maintenance costs on the basis of Arts 18 and 21 TFEU (formerly Arts 12 and 18 TEC). The CJ did state that this right was conditional on the student being sufficiently integrated into the host State. In this case, B, had been lawfully resident in the UK since 1998.

Trade union activities

Article 8, Regulation 1612/68 as amended by Regulation 312/76 deals with discrimination in the area of trade union activities.

Workers from other Member States have a right to equal treatment as regards trade union membership and the rights that go with it, for example, the right to vote and to be eligible for the administration or management posts of a trade union. They must be eligible for appointment to workers' representative bodies in the undertaking.

The provision was widely interpreted by the CJ in *ASTI v Chambre des Employés Privés* [1991], and it now applies to all bodies whose primary function is the defence and representation of workers' interests.

However, immigrant workers may, under Art 8, be excluded from taking part in the management of bodies governed by public law and from holding an office governed by public law.

HOUSING

Article 9, Regulation 1612/68 gives immigrant EU workers the right to equal treatment with regard to housing, including public housing. This would bar any rule precluding them from putting their name down, for example, for council housing.

In *Commission v Greece* [1989], the CJ held that national measures which restricted the right to own property in certain areas to Greek nationals were contrary to Art 9, Regulation 1612/68 and Art 45 TFEU (formerly Art 39 of the EC Treaty).

INDIRECT DISCRIMINATION

Article 45 TFEU (formerly Article 39 TEC) has been interpreted as prohibiting indirect as well as direct discrimination. However, indirect discrimination can be justified on objective grounds unrelated to nationality.

In cases of indirect discrimination, the CJ has approached the question in three stages:

- Does the national measure come within the scope of the Treaty?

- Is the national provision discriminatory by working to the particular disadvantage of non-nationals?

- Is it objectively justified (subject to the principle of proportionality)?

In *Allué and Coonan* [1993], the applicants were foreign language assistants at the University of Venice. They were employed on renewable fixed term contracts. This type of contract is rare in Italy and the posts in question were designed for foreign nationals. They were held to be discriminatory. The CJ held that the justifications put forward did not satisfy the principle of proportionality. There were less onerous ways of maintaining a staff-student ratio and ensuring that foreign language assistants maintained proficiency in their native tongues.

In *O'Flynn* [1996], a British regulation provided for a funeral payment. This was a means tested social benefit and was payable to cover the costs incurred by the claimant or a member of his family on the occasion of a death in the family. It was payable only if the funeral or cremation took place within the UK. The applicant was an Irish former migrant worker whose application for a payment for his son's funeral was refused on the grounds that the burial did not take place in the UK.

It was held to be indirectly discriminatory, and consequently had to be object-ively justified, subject to the principle of proportionality. The objective behind the payment was the protection of public health, and this objective should be sought even if the funeral took place outside of the UK. Purported justifications based on the cost and practical difficulties of paying the allowance were also rejected. The cost of transporting the coffin to a place distant from the deceased's home was not covered by the payment. The allowance could be fixed by reference to the cost of a reasonable burial in the UK.

The CJ also said that it was not necessary to show that the provision actually affected a substantially higher proportion of migrant workers: it was sufficient that it was likely to have such an effect.

NON-DISCRIMINATORY MEASURES AND OBJECTIVE JUSTIFICATION

The CJ confirmed in *Union Royale Belge des Sociétés de Football Association ASBL v Bosman* [1996] (see below) that Art 45 TFEU (formerly Art 39 TEC) applies to non-discriminatory measures which impede access of workers to the employment market of another Member State unless they can be objectively justified. In *Graf* [2000], the CJ held that national rules providing for compen-sation on redundancy, which did not apply if a worker voluntarily left his/her employment to take up work in another Member State, did not infringe Art 45 TFEU (formerly Art 39 TEC). The effect of the legislation on market access was 'too uncertain and indirect'.

The CJ has also recognised that Art 49 TFEU (formerly Art 43 TEC) catches non-discriminatory measures, but they may be justified on grounds of public interest. In *Gebhard* [1995], disciplinary proceedings were brought by the Milan Bar against a German lawyer for establishing himself as a lawyer on a permanent basis in Italy. He had set up chambers using the title of 'avvocato' even though he had not been admitted to the Milan Bar and his qualifications had not been formally recognised by the Italian authorities. The CJ held that in the absence of EU rules, Member States may legitimately lay down rules regulating self-employed activities. However, it added that:

'. . . national measures liable to hinder or make less attractive the exercise of fundamental freedoms guaranteed by the Treaty must fulfil four conditions: they must be applied in a non-discriminatory manner; they must be justified by imperative requirements in the general interest; they must be suitable for securing the attainment of the objective which they pursue; and they must not go beyond what is necessary in order to attain it' (para 37).

A similar approach has been adopted with regard to free movement of services: *Alpine Investments* [1995].

PRIVATE COLLECTIVE EMPLOYMENT RULES

Although Art 45 TFEU (formerly Art 39 TEC) is addressed to Member States, it was held in the case of *Walrave and Koch v Association Union Cycliste Internationale* [1974] that it was of horizontal, as well as vertical, direct effect. The case involved the rules of a sporting association which required the pacemaker of a cycling team to be of the same nationality as the other members of the team. The association was not a public or State body. It was held that Art 45 TFEU (formerly Art 39 TEC) applies, even to rules of private bodies, in respect of rules which collectively regulate employment. Sport is subject to EU law insofar as it constitutes an 'economic activity'.

In *Union Royale Belge des Sociétés de Football Association ASBL v Bosman* [1996], it was held that Art 45 TFEU (formerly Art 39 TEC) precluded the application of rules of sporting associations whereby a professional footballer could not, on the expiry of his contract, be employed by a club in another Member State unless a transfer fee was paid to the former club. It also prohibited the rules of the European football confederation (UEFA), which limited the number of professional players from another EU country that a team could field.

The CJ rejected the objective justifications that had been put forward. It had been argued that transfer fees maintain a balance between large and small clubs. The CJ felt that the system patently did not achieve this aim, as the richest clubs were able to obtain the services of the best players and the existence of financial resources was a decisive factor in the sport. The second purported justification was also rejected. This argument claimed that transfer fees gave clubs an incentive to train and develop talent. The presence of talent could not be predicted with certainty and only a limited number of players went on to play professionally.

In *Lehtonen v Fédération Royale Belge des Sociétés de Basket-ball* [2000] a Finnish basketball player was transferred to a Belgian club after the completion of the 1995–96 Finnish championship. The player was fielded during the later stages of the Belgian championship of the same year. The Belgian club was penalised as the transfer had taken place after the FIBA deadline for transfers of players within the European zone (there were different deadlines for international transfers). The deadline was justified by FIBA as a means of preventing undue disruption of national championships by late transfers. The court ruled that this type of deadline could possibly be justified on the grounds of public interest, but that the deadlines for European transfers and non-member transfers would have to be the same.

Surprisingly, it is only relatively recently that the Court has been asked to decide whether Art 45 TFEU (formerly Art 39 TEC) has 'full' horizontal direct effect; that is, whether it can be relied upon against a private employer. In *Angonese* [2000], the Court held that it can. When A, an Italian national, applied for a job with a bank in the Italian city of Bolzano he was unsuccessful because one of the conditions of entry was possession of a special certificate (issued only by the local authorities) confirming bilingualism in German and Italian. A, who had studied languages at the University of Vienna, contended that his degree certificate should be acceptable and refusal to accept it would constitute indirect discrimination contrary to Art 45 TFEU (formerly Art 39 TEC). The CJ agreed.

EXCEPTIONS

Article 45(3), 52 and 62 TFEU (formerly Articles 39(3), 46 and 55 TEC) allow an exception from the free movement provisions where it is justified on grounds of public policy, public security or public health.

These derogations are further fleshed out by Directive 2004/38 (which repeals Directive 64/221) and incorporates much of the former case law which is, therefore, considered below.

MEANING OF 'PUBLIC POLICY'

In *Van Duyn v Home Office* [1974], it was said that the concept of public policy is subject to control by Union institutions but that the definition of public policy can vary from State to State.

In *Rutili v French Minister of the Interior* [1975], it was held that for the public policy exception to be invoked, the threat must be genuine and serious. Restrictions are subject to the proportionality principle.

In *R v Bouchereau* [1977], the test was expressed as: '. . . a genuine and sufficiently serious threat to the requirements of public policy affecting one of the fundamental principles of society'.

MEANING OF 'PUBLIC SECURITY'

This is reserved for serious crimes and subversive, anti-State activities, (e.g. terrorism or espionage). Public security was specifically referred to in *Otieza Olazabal* [2002], involving a member of ETA (*Euskadi Ta Askatasuna* (Basque Homeland and Freedom)). The case involved a Spanish national threatened with deportation from France following conviction of terrorism offences. The CJ dealt with it as a case of 'public security', stating:

> The defendant in the main proceedings . . . has been sentenced in France to 18 months' imprisonment and a four-year ban on residence for conspiracy to disturb public order by intimidation or terror . . . he formed part of an armed and organised group whose activity constitutes a threat to public order in French territory. Prevention of such activity may, moreover, be regarded as falling within the maintenance of public security.

Personal conduct and criminal convictions

Article 27(2) of Directive 2004/38 states that 'measures taken on grounds of public policy or public security shall comply with the principle of proportionality and shall be based exclusively on the personal conduct of the individual concerned'.

It continues that previous criminal convictions shall not in themselves constitute grounds for taking such measures. The personal conduct of the individual concerned must represent a genuine, present and sufficiently serious threat affecting one of the fundamental interests of society.

Article 27(1) states that 'the grounds shall not be invoked to serve economic ends'.

Cases on the meaning of personal conduct and the effect of criminal convictions

In *Van Duyn v Home Office* [1974], it was held that present association with a group or organisation could count towards personal conduct, but that past association could never do so.

Van Duyn was a Dutch national, who was refused entry into the UK on grounds of public policy. She wished to take up employment with the Church of Scientology. Scientology was not illegal but was considered socially undesirable by the UK Government. The refusal was based on personal conduct due to the applicant's association with the Scientology sect. The case was the first preliminary reference made by a court of the UK, and the controversial result has been explained as an attempt by the CJ to be accommodating to the UK on its first reference.

The CJ held that conduct does not have to be illegal to justify exclusion but must be socially harmful, and administrative measures must have been taken to counteract activities.

▶ VAN DUYN [1974]

Ms Van Duyn was a Dutch national and a member of the Church of Scientology. She was refused entry to work for the College of Scientology in the UK.

The CJ held that present membership of an organisation, against which administrative measures had been taken, did constitute personal conduct for the purposes of Art 45(3) TFEU (formerly Art 39(3) TEC).

The CJ has, after *Van Duyn*, laid down much stricter tests. In *R v Bouchereau* [1977], a French national, resident in the UK, who had twice been convicted of drugs offences, was threatened with deportation from the UK. It was held that previous convictions should only be taken into account if there was a present threat to requirements of public policy, but past conduct alone could constitute a threat if it was sufficiently grave.

▶ BOUCHEREAU [1977]

Bouchereau, a French citizen, working in the UK, was given a suspended sentence for a drug offence.

The CJ held that measures to deport him could only be taken if he posed a genuine and serious threat to society.

In *Adoui and Cornuaille* [1982], two French waitresses were working in a bar in Belgium but were also working as prostitutes. Prostitution was legal in Belgium but was discouraged. The Belgian authorities denied them a residence permit.

It was held that Member States could not deny residence to non-nationals because of conduct which, when attributable to a State's own nationals, did not give rise to repressive measures or other genuine and effective measures to combat such conduct.

▶ ADOUI AND CORNUAILLE [1982]

French prostitutes could not be denied entry to Belgium where prostitution was not illegal.

The correctness of the decision in *Adoui and Cornuaille* was confirmed in *Jany and Others* [2001]. The case concerned a number of female prostitutes from the Czech Republic who were working in Amsterdam. They successfully resisted deportation on the basis that the Dutch authorities' attitude to similar activities on the part of their own nationals did not attract repressive measures.

In *Bonsignore* [1975], an Italian living in Germany was threatened with deportation after conviction of a criminal offence as a deterrent. It was held that a deportation order can be made only in connection with breaches of peace and public security which may be committed by the individual concerned.

Similar issues arose in *Calfa* [1999]. C, an Italian national, was convicted for possession and use of prohibited drugs whilst in Greece. A Greek court expelled her for life from Greece, as required by Greek law. C appealed against the expulsion, arguing that Greece was not empowered to expel a national of another Member State for life if a comparable measure could not be taken against a Greek citizen. The CJ agreed: automatic expulsion (without any account being taken of the personal conduct of the offender or of the danger that that person represented) was contrary to the 'personal conduct' requirement in Art 3(1) of Directive 64/221. (See now Art 27 of Dir 2004/38.)

The decision on 'personal conduct' in *Orfanopoulos* [2004], involving provisions of German law very similar to that in *Calfa*, providing for automatic deportation of foreign nationals convicted of certain drugs and public order offences. The CJ held that:

'Community law precludes the deportation of a national of a Member State . . . *where such measure automatically follows a criminal conviction*, without any account being taken of the personal conduct of the offender or of the danger which that person represents for the requirements of public policy.'

PROTECTION AGAINST EXPULSION

Article 28 of Directive 2004/38 provides that before taking an expulsion decision on grounds of public policy or public security, the host Member State shall take account of considerations such as how long the individual concerned has resided on its territory, his/her age, state of health, family and economic situation, social and cultural integration into the host Member State and the extent of his/her links with the country of origin.

Even under the former law, the significance of the individual having a family in the host Member State was taken into account.

Significance of the individual having a family

In *Orfanopoulos* [2004], a Greek national had married a German woman and they had three children. He was a repeat drugs offender who had spent several years in and out of German prisons and drug rehabilitation clinics before eventually facing deportation. The CJ was asked what significance, if any, his factual situation had on the German authorities' entitlement to pursue deportation. The Court decided (having made reference to the right to respect for a family life, protected by Article 8 of the European Convention of Human Rights) that it was a relevant factor:

It is clear that the removal of a person from the country where close members of his family are living may amount to an infringement of

> the right to respect for family life . . . account must be taken, particularly, of the nature and seriousness of the offences committed by the person concerned, the length of his residence in the host Member State, the period which has elapsed since the commission of the offence, the family circumstances of the person concerned and the seriousness of the difficulties which the spouse and any of their children risk facing in the country of origin of the person concerned.

This does not, of course, say that an individual who happens to be married to a national of the host State cannot be deported; but it does say that a person is entitled to have his or her 'family circumstances' taken into account.

PUBLIC HEALTH

Under Art 29(1) of Directive 2004/38, the only diseases which can justify restricting the right of entry and residence on the ground of public health are those with epidemic potential as defined by the World Health Organisation and other infectious diseases or other contagious parasitic diseases if they are subject to protection provisions applying to nationals of the host Member State.

PROCEDURAL PROTECTION

This is now contained in Articles 30–33 of Directive 2004/38. Briefly Art 30 is concerned with notification of decisions and requires the persons concerned to be notified in writing of any decision taken under Art 27(1) above. They are required to be informed precisely and in full of the public policy, public security or public health grounds on which the decision in their case is based, unless this is contrary to the interests of State security. The notification must also specify the court or administrative body to which they may appeal. Except in cases of urgency, the time allowed to leave the host Member State shall be not less than one month from the date of notification.

Article 31 provides procedural safeguards and gives detail of access to judicial and administrative redress procedures in the host Member State. Article 32 deals with the duration of exclusion orders and Art 33 stipulates that expulsion orders may not be issued by the host Member State as a penalty other than in circumstances which fulfil the conditions set out in Arts 27–29.

PUBLIC SERVICE EXEMPTION

Free movement of workers does not apply to public service under Art 45(4) TFEU (formerly Art 39(4) TEC). This could be a very significant exemption, but has been interpreted narrowly.

In *Commission v Belgium (Re Public Employees)* [1979], all posts in the 'public service' were limited to Belgian nationals. The Belgian Government argued that those jobs were within the public service. The CJ held that it only applied to the exercise of official authority and to employees who were safeguarding the general interests of the State.

> ▶ **COMMISSION v BELGIUM (Re Public Employees) [1979]**
>
> **Belgian law reserved posts in the public service for Belgian nationals only.**
>
> The CJ ruled that the public service exception applied only to posts which involved 'direct or indirect participation in the exercise of powers conferred by public law and duties designed to safeguard the general interests of the state'.

Where the 'public service' derogation does apply, then Member States are free to exclude foreign nationals altogether. In *Anker v Germany* [2003], the CJ held that provisions of German law restricting the position of ship's master to German nationals was justifiable in principle on the basis that ships' masters had responsibility for maintaining public order on the ship; they also had powers in respect of marriages and deaths occurring on board. The CJ did qualify its judgment by holding that:

> The scope of [Art 45(4) TFEU (formerly Art 39(4) TEC)] must be limited to what is strictly necessary for safeguarding the general interests of the Member State concerned, which cannot be imperilled if rights under powers conferred by public law are exercised only sporadically, even exceptionally, by nationals of other Member States.

Other occupations where the derogation may apply would seem to be the security services (in the UK that is MI5 and MI6), the armed forces, the higher echelons of the civil service, the police force, and so on. Indeed, in the UK membership of the British Army's fighting units is restricted to British, Irish and Commonwealth nationals.

A similar exemption applies in relation to the self-employed and the provision of services. Art 49 TFEU (formerly Art 45 TEC) states that the '. . . provisions of this chapter shall not apply, so far as any given Member State is concerned, to activities which in that state are connected, even occasionally, with the exercise of official authority.' Art 55 states that this exemption should also be applied to Art 56 TFEU (formerly Art 49 TEC). The CJ has adopted a narrow interpretation of the exemption: *Reyners* [1974].

MUTUAL RECOGNITION OF QUALIFICATIONS

The obligations on Member States to remove barriers to trade contained in Arts 45, 49 and 56 TFEU (formerly Arts 39, 43 and 49 TEC) are a means of negative integration. The political institutions have also enacted secondary legislation in these fields designed to harmonise national rules which restrict access to occupations and professions. This is known as positive integration and has been incremental in nature. The initial approach of the EU legislature was to enact harmonising measures separately for each economic activity or profession and setting minimum training requirements. This approach was too slow and cumbersome. In the 1980s, the Community switched to a system of general mutual recognition and adopted several directives providing for the mutual recognition of qualifications: Dir 89/48 (Mutual Recognition of Diplomas) provided for the mutual recognition of higher-education diplomas awarded on completion of professional education and training of at least three years' duration; Dir 92/51 (Mutual Recognition of Diplomas for other Professional Activities) covered education and training other than three year higher-education diplomas. Both were amended by Dir 2001/19.

Directive 2005/36 (Recognition of Professional Qualifications) now replaces all earlier directives (three mutual recognition directives and twelve sectoral directives) in order to consolidate the existing law into a coherent legislative framework. The basic principle contained in the Directive is that of mutual recognition whereby Member States investigate whether a particular qualification or experience is equivalent to that applicable in the host Member State. If so, an individual may carry out their profession. If not, the Member State may require an aptitude test or adaptation period to be completed.

PROTECTION OF WORKERS AND EMPLOYEES

On 19 November 2008 the Directive 2008/104/EC on temporary agency workers was adopted and must be implemented by Member States by 5 December 2011. The aim of this Directive is:

> to ensure the protection of temporary agency workers and to improve the quality of temporary agency work by ensuring that the principle of equal treatment, as set out in Article 5, is applied to temporary agency workers, and by recognising temporary work agencies as employers, while taking into account the need to establish a suitable framework for the use of temporary agency work with a view to contributing effectively to the creation of jobs and to the development of flexible forms of working. (See Art. 2.)

On 22 October 2008 Directive 2008/94/EC on the protection of employees in the event of the insolvency of their employer was adopted. It provides that:

> It is necessary to provide for the protection of employees in the event of the insolvency of their employer and to ensure a minimum degree of protection, in particular in order to guarantee payment of their outstanding claims, while taking account of the need for balanced economic and social development in the Community. (See para 3.)

APPLICATION OF LAW ON FREE MOVEMENT OF PERSONS AND CITIZENSHIP
(1) Identify which category of persons may benefit from the right to free movement.
(2) Identify the rights to which each category of persons is entitled.
(3) Identify whether the host Member State may derogate from these rights and the procedural safeguards which apply.

You should now be confident that you would be able to tick all of the boxes on the checklist at the beginning of this chapter. To check your knowledge of Free movement of persons and citizenship why not visit the companion website and take the Multiple Choice Question test. Check your understanding of the terms and vocabulary used in this chapter with the flashcard glossary.

6

EU sex equality legislation

Explain the scope of Art 157 TFEU (formerly Art 141 of the EC Treaty) ▪

Discuss the provisions of the Equal Treatment Directive 2006/54 in relation to equal pay and equal treatment ▪

Give examples of the rulings of the CJ in cases on equal pay and equal treatment ▪

FREEDOM FROM DISCRIMINATION

From the outset, it is important to distinguish between direct discrimination and indirect discrimination. These concepts are both defined in the Equal Treatment Directive 2006/54. Direct discrimination is where one person is treated less favourably, on grounds of sex, than another is, has been, or would be treated in a comparable situation. Indirect discrimination is where an apparently neutral provision, criterion or practice would put persons of one sex at a particular disadvantage compared with persons of the other sex, unless that provision, etc. is objectively justified by a legitimate aim, and the means of achieving that aim are appropriate and necessary.

The directive also provides that discrimination includes harassment and sexual harassment, as well as any less favourable treatment based on a person's rejection of or submission to such conduct and any instruction to discriminate against persons on grounds of sex.

The Equal Treatment Directive 2006/54 is a consolidating directive, replacing the Equal Pay Directive 75/117 and the Equal Treatment Directive 76/207. The new directive incorporates many rulings of the CJ and, therefore, much former case law is included below. It does not introduce any substantially new amendments.

Briefly, therefore, it governs:

- equal treatment in access to employment and promotion;
- vocational training;
- working conditions, including pay;
- occupational social security.

EQUAL PAY – THE LEGISLATIVE FRAMEWORK

Article 157 TFEU (formerly Art 141 TEC) provides that each Member State shall ensure that the principle of equal pay for male and female workers for equal work or work of equal value is applied.

The Equal Pay Directive 75/117, which fleshed out the provisions of Art 157 TFEU (formerly Art 141 TEC), has now been repealed and replaced by Directive 2006/54, which incorporates much of the former case law on pay.

ARTICLE 157 TFEU

Direct effect of Art 157 TFEU

Article 157 TFEU, which established the principle of equal pay for men and women, has direct effect, that is, it creates rights and obligations for individuals which may be enforced in national courts.

In *Defrenne v SABENA (No 2)* [1976], the CJ held that Art 157 TFEU (119 TEC) had horizontal and vertical direct effect.

In the interests of legal certainty, the effect of the judgment was limited, so that claims for backdated pay could only be made from the date of judgment, unless a claim had already been brought.

What is 'pay' for the purposes of Art 157 TFEU?

Pay is defined as the 'ordinary basic minimum wage or salary' plus 'any other consideration', whether in cash or in kind, which the worker receives directly or indirectly in respect of his employment from his employer (Article 157(2) TFEU).

State pension schemes

In *Defrenne v Belgium (No 1)* [1971] the CJ ruled that social security schemes or benefits, in particular retirement pensions, directly governed by legislation without any elements within the undertaking which apply to general categories of workers, fall outside the meaning of 'pay' for the purposes of Art 157 TFEU.

Criticisms of *Defrenne (No 1)* test:

- it discriminates between employees whose employers operate one form of pension scheme rather than another;

- the operation of Art 157 TFEU may be dependent on the national organisation of pension schemes.

The first of a number of exceptions to *Defrenne (No 1)* was laid down in *Liefting* [1984]. Contributions to a State social security scheme affected the level of gross pay, and, therefore, the level of other benefits did constitute 'pay' for the purpose of Art 157 TFEU.

Article 157 TFEU was again held to be applicable to a statutory social security benefit in *Rinner-Kühn* [1989]. In this case, statutory sick pay in the form of wages which an employer was required to pay by law in the event of illness was held to be 'pay'. The employer was required to continue paying an employee who was incapable of working for a period of up to six weeks. Thereafter, the social security system paid 80 per cent of the normal earnings of a worker. The case is hard to distinguish from *Defrenne (No 1)* and yet the opposite conclusion was reached. This has created uncertainty as to the true state of the law. National legislation which allowed employers to maintain a global difference between two categories of worker, part time and full time, was contrary to Art 157 TFEU. It also fell within Art 157 TFEU as it arose from the employment relationship. As part time workers were predominantly female, it constituted indirect discrimination and had to be objectively justified.

Occupational pensions

A further area of difficulty has been occupational pension schemes. Many occupational pension schemes operate in addition to a State scheme, have some State support and in some cases are organised by the State.

Directive 86/378 on the implementation of the principle of equal treatment for men and women in occupational social security schemes showed that the Council considered occupational pensions to be more a matter of social security rather than pay.

However, the CJ took a different view in *Bilka-Kaufhaus v Karin Weber von Hartz* [1986] in which it held that an occupational pension entirely financed by the employer was within Art 157 TFEU. The scheme was adopted in accordance with German legislation applicable to such pension schemes but it had been set up voluntarily through the agreement between Bilka and the staff committee representing its employees. It was a contractual rather than a statutory scheme and was financed entirely by the employer. This led the CJ to hold that the pension was capable of constituting 'pay' under Art 157 TFEU.

This interpretation has clearly affected the relationship between Art 157 TFEU and Directive 86/378. By concluding that Art 157 TFEU could apply to occupational social security schemes, the Directive is largely redundant and is of use only in relation to indirect discrimination. This re-ordering of the frontier between Art 157 and the secondary legislation relating to equality has advantages for applicants, as Art 157 TFEU has both vertical and horizontal direct effect.

The way in which pensions were organised in the UK has caused particular difficulties with regard to Art 157 TFEU. The UK provided for an additional State pension in addition to the basic retirement pension in the form of a State Earnings Related Pension Scheme (SERPS). This allowed for a supplementary State pension related to earnings in addition to the basic pension. However, the cost of the scheme proved to be prohibitive and the Government sought to privatise this supplemental pension in the form of 'contracting out'.

The issue then arose as to whether these 'contracted out' pensions were within or outside Art 157 TFEU. The answer came in *Barber v Guardian Royal Exchange Assurance Group* [1990]. Barber was an employee of the defendants and was made redundant at the age of 52. His occupational pension was a contracted out scheme and he claimed that it was in breach of Art 157 TFEU. A woman would have been entitled to an immediate pension at the age of 50, whereas a man had to wait until 55 before receiving his pension. Barber had suffered a detriment by waiting longer for his pension on grounds of his sex. In addition, the statutory redundancy scheme which was also payable at different ages for men and women was challenged.

The CJ held that Art 157 TFEU applied to contracted out occupational pension schemes and to all redundancy payments. The CJ pointed out that the pension scheme in *Defrenne (No 1)* had been determined less by the employment relationship than by considerations of social policy. Art 157 TFEU cannot encompass social security schemes or benefits, directly governed by legislation without any element of agreement within the undertaking or occupational branch concerned, which are compulsorily applicable to general categories of worker. By contrast, contracted out schemes are the result either of an agreement between the workers or employers or of a unilateral decision of the employer. They are wholly financed by the employer or by both the employer and employees, without any contribution by the public authorities in any circumstances.

Contracted out schemes are not applicable to general categories of worker but apply to workers employed by certain undertakings. Although such schemes are established in conformity with national legislation, they are governed by their own rules.

The Court of Justice recognised that the judgment in *Barber* might cause confusion, not least because of the existence of Art 9, Directive 86/378. *Barber* illustrates how the CJ has moved the frontiers between Art 157 TFEU and secondary legislation.

There were also misgivings about the cost of implementing the judgment. It was thought to be particularly expensive in the Netherlands and the UK because of the way in which their pensions industries were organised. The UK pensions industry warned that it would cost £50 billion to implement.

As a result, the CJ placed a temporal limitation on *Barber* that the judgment could not be applied retrospectively. Consequently, with the exception of actions already pending, no claim could be brought for pension benefits for the period before the date of judgment on 17 May 1990. Although the justification for this temporal limitation was based on legal certainty, it was also influenced by costs considerations.

This temporal limitation caused considerable confusion. Did it mean that contributions payable after 17 May 1990 had to be equal or did it mean that the benefits received after that date had to be equal? If it meant the latter, then contributions made on an unequal basis before 17 May 1990 would have to be equalised. The Member States sought to restrict the temporal effects of the *Barber* judgment in a Protocol to the Treaty on European Union:

> ... benefits under occupational pension schemes shall not be considered as remuneration if and in so far as they are attributable to periods of employment prior to 17 May 1990.

This has led to further criticism that the Member States were using their legislative function to usurp the interpretative function of the CJ. A crisis between the institutions of the Union was averted by the case of *Ten Oever* [1993]. Equality of treatment may be claimed only in relation to benefits payable in respect of periods of employment subsequent to 17 May 1990. It was also held that benefits paid to an employee's survivor were within Art 157 TFEU (formerly Art 141 EC), since the benefit was paid by reason of the employment relationship. The case of *Newstead* would now appear to be weak authority.

Further clarification of the *Barber* judgment was obtained in *Coloroll Pension Trustees Ltd v Russell* [1994]. It was held that Art 157 TFEU applied to pensions paid under a trust, even though pension fund trustees are not parties to the employment relationship. Trustees are still under this obligation to observe Art 157, even if this is contrary to the trust deed. The equal treatment principle also applies to employers who have transferred their acquired rights from another pension fund which has not observed Art 157 TFEU. This means that pension fund trustees may have to make good the cost of another company failing to comply with Art 157 TFEU.

The case of *Beune* [1994] again raised the issue of whether a pension was within Art 157 TFEU as a result of being part of the employment relationship, or whether it was part of social policy and, therefore, governed by Directive 79/7. This involved civil service pensions, and the CJ held that, even where a pension was affected by 'considerations of social policy, of State organisation, or of the ethics or even of budgetary considerations', which could point to being classed as social security, it could still be classed as pay and consequently come within Art 157 TFEU, even though the pension is paid by a public employer, so long as:

■ it concerned a particular category of worker rather than general categories;

■ it was directly related to the period of service;

■ its amount was calculated by reference to the employee's last salary.

The case of *Neath v Hugh Steeper Ltd* [1993] revolved around a 'defined benefit' scheme. In such a scheme, the criteria for the pension are fixed in advance and are fixed as a fraction of the final year's salary for each year of service. Employee contributions must be the same for men and women. However, employer contributions can vary over time. This was the result of using sex based actuarial factors, as the pensions actually paid would vary. Statistically, women live longer than men, and hence the pension is needed for a longer period. A number of objections can be made to this. First, it treats individual employees on the basis of stereotypical assumptions. Secondly, a man could receive less in the event of a capital sum on redundancy, transfer benefits or a deferred pension. The CJ held that the employer contributions were not 'pay' within the meaning of Art 157 TFEU. The contributions were made to ensure an adequate pension.

In *Roberts v Birds Eye Walls Ltd* [1993], Mrs Roberts was forced to retire early on grounds of ill health. She received a bridging pension as part of an occupational pension scheme. The payment was made *ex gratia* and its aim was to place employees in the same financial position they would have been in if they had not been forced to take early retirement. Women received the State pension aged 60, whereas men had to wait until the age of 65. The bridging pension paid to women between the ages of 60 and 65 was lower than that for men, as the employers took into account the State pension. Women consequently needed less to bring them up to the financial position they were in whilst working.

The CJ found that the purpose of the bridging pension was to maintain the level of income. Consequently, the CJ did not find the decision discriminatory. This decision was recently confirmed in *Hlozek* [2004], another case involving bridging pensions.

To conclude, having broadened the concept of 'pay' in *Barber*, the CJ drew back in *Neath* and other post-*Barber* cases. The outcome of these post-*Barber* cases with all their anomalies is now contained in Title II – Chapter 2 of the consolidating Equal Treatment Directive 2006/54.

Other examples of what constitutes pay

In *Gillespie v Northern Health and Social Services Board* [1996], the applicants' maternity pay was calculated by reference to the last two pay cheques prior to taking maternity leave. They received full pay for four weeks, nine-tenths of full weekly pay for a further two weeks thereafter, and then half pay for 12 weeks. Whilst on maternity leave, a pay rise was awarded which was backdated, but the applicants did not receive the benefit of this pay rise. The applicants claimed discrimination, first, on the grounds that their pay had been reduced during maternity leave and, secondly, on grounds that they had not received the benefit of the backdated pay rise. It was held that neither Art 157 TFEU nor the Equal Pay Directive (75/117 (see below)) required the women to receive full pay during their maternity leave, provided that the amount was not so low as to jeopardise the purpose of maternity leave. However, the applicants were entitled to pay rises awarded between the start of the payment of maternity pay and the end of maternity leave.

The Alabaster *case*

Gillespie was followed in *Alabaster v Woolwich Building Society* [2004], a case which attracted considerable publicity at the time. Ms Alabaster worked for the Woolwich between December 1987 and August 1996. In January 1996 she went on maternity leave. In December 1995, she had been awarded a pay rise, but her maternity pay was calculated on the basis of her salary in October 1995. The pay-rise was not back-dated. Ms Alabaster argued that the failure to take account of her salary increase was contrary to Art 157 TFEU. The CJ agreed: had she not gone on maternity leave, she would have received the full benefit of the pay rise throughout her period of maternity leave. Therefore, to refuse to acknowledge the pay rise in calculating maternity pay constituted a breach of Article 157 TFEU.

This case law is now reflected in Article 15 of the Directive 2006/54, which provides that a woman on maternity leave shall be entitled, after the end of her period of maternity leave, to return to her job or to an equivalent post on terms and conditions which are no less favourable to her and to benefit from any improvement in working conditions to which she would have been entitled during her absence.

Article 157 TFEU does not apply to working conditions

In *Defrenne v SABENA (No 3)* [1979], it was held that Art 157 TFEU does not stretch to equality of working conditions other than pay between men and women. Consequently, an attempt to use Art 157 TFEU as a means of ensuring equality of retirement ages under Art 157 TFEU failed.

Similarly, in *Burton v British Railways Board* [1982], access to a voluntary early retirement redundancy scheme, where women could apply earlier than men, was governed by the Equal Treatment Directive and not by Art 157 TFEU.

'Pay' includes non-contractual benefits

Benefits need only be granted in respect of employment to come within Art 157 TFEU and do not have to arise from a contractual relationship: *Garland v British Rail Engineering Ltd* [1982]. Special travel facilities provided to retired male workers and their families, which are not available to retired female employees and their families, are 'pay' within Art 157 TFEU.

Transparency and the burden of proof

In the case of *Enderby v Frenchay HA* [1993], the claimant was a speech therapist and her profession was overwhelmingly dominated by females. She claimed that members of her profession were discriminated against by being paid less well than clinical psychologists and pharmacists. The work performed by these professions were of equal value to hers, and consisted mainly of men. The CJ held that normally the person alleging discrimination, that is, the worker, must prove it, but where a *prima facie* case of discrimination exists it is for the *employer* to show that there are objective reasons for the difference in pay. The fact that the difference has been caused by separate collective bargaining processes cannot be sufficient objective justification. It was for the national court to determine whether difficulties in recruitment constituted objective justification.

A similar conclusion was also reached in *Handels- og Kontorfunktionaerernes Forbund i Danmark v Dansk Arbejdsgiverforening ex p Danfoss* [1989]. Danfoss had paid the same basic wage to employees in the same group, but it also awarded individual pay supplements, which were calculated on the basis of mobility, training and seniority. These criteria were likely to disadvantage women, as they tended to have greater restrictions on their mobility and less seniority due to domestic caring duties for which they were still disproportionately responsible. The case had been brought by two female employees who had received 7 per cent less pay than male workers in the same wage group. The CJ held that, where an undertaking applies a system of pay that is lacking in transparency, it is for the employer to show that the wages system is not discriminatory if a female worker establishes a *prima facie* case by showing that, in relation to a large number of employees, the average pay for women is less than men.

Transparency was also an issue in the *Royal Copenhagen* case [1995]. The complaint was that Royal Copenhagen's blue pattern painters, who were predominantly women, were paid less than automatic machine operators, who were exclusively men. The pay consisted of a fixed element and a variable element. The fixed element was not the same for the different groups of workers but the union asserted that the different work was of equal value. The variable element consisted of piece work which varied according to the output of each individual worker. It was held that Art 157 TFEU (formerly Art 141 TEC) applied to these piece work pay schemes. The mere finding that in a piece work pay scheme the average pay of a group of workers consisting mainly of women was appreciably lower than the average pay of a group of workers consisting predominantly of men carrying out work to which equal value was attributed was not sufficient to establish discrimination with regard to 'pay'.

However, where it was not possible to identify the factors determining the variable elements, the employer might have to bear the burden of proving that the differences in pay were not due to discrimination. Otherwise, the workers might be deprived of any effective means of enforcing the principle of equal pay. The pay differential would not constitute discrimination if it could be objectively justified.

In comparing the average pay of the two groups, the groups chosen had to comprise a relatively large number of workers so as to ensure that differences in pay were not due to fortuitous or short term factors or to differences in workers' individual output.

The CJ restated the principle that there should be equal pay where the elements of pay were determined by collective bargaining. However, the national court could take into account whether the differences in pay were objectively justified.

Note that Art 19 of the Equal Treatment Directive 2006/54 specifically requires Member States to ensure that, where an employee establishes facts from which it may be presumed that there has been direct or indirect discrimination, it is for the respondent employer to prove that there has been no breach of the principle of equal treatment.

PART TIME WORKERS

The cases relating to part time workers have developed the law relating to indirect discrimination. Provisions which treat part time workers adversely are not *prima facie* discriminatory, as they affect both sexes. However, as part time workers are predominantly women, such provisions will have a greater adverse impact on them.

In *Jenkins v Kingsgate (Clothing Productions) Ltd* [1981], it was held that a variation in pay between full time and part time workers does not breach Art 157 TFEU, provided the hourly rates are applied without distinction based on sex, and differences are 'objectively justified'. This imported the concept of the employer's intention. It is rarely the employer's intention to discriminate: it is rather to gain a commercial advantage through the use of cheap labour. *Jenkins* was interpreted by English courts as meaning that, if the employer was motivated by commercial advantage, then that objectively justified discrimination. This would have made it difficult for part time workers to succeed under Art 157 TFEU.

The effects of *Jenkins* were mitigated by *Bilka-Kaufhaus*: the CJ held that it is for a national court to determine whether a policy is objectively justified, but it was limited by the principle of proportionality. The employer has to show that the policy:

■ met a genuine need of the enterprise;

■ was suitable for attaining the objective set;

■ was necessary for the purpose.

Rinner-Kühn is also significant in that, although the question of objective justification is left to national courts, the CJ is prepared to set down limits as to what can constitute justification. In particular, it will look at the merits of justification arguments. So, in *Rinner-Kühn,* the German Government could not argue that part time workers are less dependent on their earnings than full time workers.

Significant guidance as to the merits of objective justification arguments, in relation to small employers, was provided by the CJ in a case under the Equal Treatment Directive (76/207) in *Kirsammer-Hack v Sidal* [1993], where it was held that exclusion from employment protection for part time employees of firms which had fewer than five employees was objectively justified on the ground that it lightened the administrative, financial and legal burdens on small firms.

Two German cases have also extended the rights of part time workers. In *Kowalska v Freie und Hansestadt Hamburg* [1990], it was held that a provision of a collective agreement excluding part time workers from severance pay infringed Art 157 (formerly Art 141 TEC). The Court also held that the national court must amend indirectly discriminatory provisions of collective agreements, as opposed to simply declaring them void.

In *Nimz v Freie und Hansestadt Hamburg* [1991], part time workers had to work twice as long for reclassification to a higher grade than full time workers. The CJ held that, in showing that experience is an objective factor which leads to improvement in performance, it would have to be shown that additional experience leads to better performance in the job.

The limitation of the temporal effects of *Barber* does not apply to the right to join an occupational pension scheme or to the right to payment of a retirement pension where the worker was excluded from the scheme in breach of Art 157 TFEU.

Consequently, part time workers have the right to join a pension scheme unless their exclusion can be objectively justified (*Vroege v NCIV* [1994]). Furthermore, this right can be backdated to 8 April 1976, which is the date of the judgment of *Defrenne (No 2)*. However, it was held in *Fisscher* [1994] that, where a pension scheme requires them, contributions can be demanded from an employee who wishes to backdate membership of the scheme for that period.

These principles were again stated in *Dietz* [1996]. The applicant, who was employed for seven hours a week, could exercise these rights directly against the administrator of the scheme, but the employee had to pay contributions for the period concerned.

SCOPE OF ART 157 TFEU

Article 157 TFEU does not cover discrimination on grounds of sexual orientation. It was held in *Grant v South West Trains* [1998] that neither Art 157 TFEU nor the Equal Pay Directive, Directive 75/117, covered discrimination on grounds of sexual orientation. The defendant employer had provided benefits in kind to employees in the form of travel concessions for spouses and opposite sex partners of employees but not same sex partners.

The decision, unsurprisingly, attracted a considerable amount of attention both in the media and in the legal community at the time. However, *Grant* is of largely historical interest now, following the adoption by the Council of Directive 2000/78, which prohibits, *inter alia*, sexual orientation discrimination in the employment context throughout the Union. (The Directive has been implemented into UK law by the Employment Equality (Sexual Orientation) Regulations 2003, which came into force on 1 December 2003.)

The judgment in *Grant* did not follow Advocate General Elmer's opinion and was surprising in the light of the CJ's ruling in *P v S and Cornwall CC* [1996]. In that case, a post-operative transsexual was dismissed from her employment as a consequence of her transsexualism. The CJ applied a purposive interpretation to Art 2(1), Directive 76/207 (the Equal Treatment Directive) and argued that the purpose of the rights it intended to protect covered gender reassignment.

Grant was not brought on the basis of Directive 76/207 and the CJ declined to give a purposive interpretation. The judgment referred to the Treaty of Amsterdam, which gives the EC powers in the field of discrimination on grounds of sexual orientation. The CJ felt that it was up to the Council to pass secondary legislation to give effect to these rights, which it has now done.

WHAT IS EQUAL WORK?
Article 157 TFEU is not limited to situations where the man and woman are contemporaneously employed. In *Macarthys v Smith* [1980], the applicant was paid less for the same job as her male predecessor. The CJ also rejected the need for the adoption of a 'hypothetical male': the parallels could be drawn on the basis of 'concrete appraisals of work actually performed by employees of different sex within the establishment or service'.

'Equal work' enables applicants to compare themselves to other groups of workers who have had their work rated as inferior but still receive more pay (*Murphy v An Bord Telecom Eireann* [1987]).

EQUAL TREATMENT DIRECTIVE 2006/54 – TITLE II – EQUAL PAY

As mentioned above, Directive 2006/54 is a consolidating directive and replaces the Equal Pay Directive 75/117.

Article 4 of the Directive prohibits discrimination and states 'For the same work or for work to which equal value is attributed, direct and indirect discrimination on grounds of sex with regard to all aspects and conditions of remuneration shall be eliminated'.

Article 14 of the Directive provides 'there shall be no direct or indirect discrimination on grounds of sex in the public or private sectors regarding employment and working conditions, including dismissal, as well as pay as provided for in Article 141 of the Treaty (now 157 TFEU)'.

If a national court can identify discrimination solely by reference to Art 157 TFEU, it will be directly effective. This is important because the Treaty article can be invoked both vertically and horizontally (i.e. against private employers), thus avoiding any problems which might arise regarding the direct effect of the directive.

Article 4 of the Directive continues that where a job classification system is used for determining pay, it shall be based on the same criteria for both men and women and so drawn up as to exclude any discrimination on grounds of sex.

You will remember that under the Directive, the respondent employer bears the burden of proof once the claimant employee has established facts from which it may be presumed that there has been direct or indirect discrimination.

Cases decided under the Equal Pay Directive 75/117 are now considered.

It was held in *Angestelltenbetriebsrat der Wiener Gebietskrankenkasse v Wiener Gebietskrankenkasse* [1999] that 'same work' in Art 1, Directive 75/117 and Art 157 TFEU (formerly Art 141 TEC) did not apply to two groups of psychotherapists. One group held degrees in psychology, the other group were paid more and had trained as doctors. The difference in training could be an objective justification for difference in pay.

Initially, the UK implemented measures that defined equal pay as 'like work' and 'work was rated as equivalent' on the basis of a job evaluation undertaken with the consent of an employer. This was held to be a breach of the Directive in Case 61/81 *Commission v UK* [1981], as there had been a failure to provide a means whereby claims of equal value might be assessed in the absence of a job evaluation scheme. As a result, the Equal Pay (Amendment) Regulations 1983 were passed and an employment tribunal now has the power to have a report prepared to determine whether something is of equal value.

Case 143/83 *Commission v Denmark* [1983] allows for comparisons to be made with work of equal value in different establishments which are covered by the same collective agreement.

In *Rummler v Dato-Druck GmbH* [1987], a job evaluation scheme was challenged as the criteria it assessed included, *inter alia*, muscular effort. This was held not to be discriminatory so long as:

- the system as a whole precluded discrimination;

- the criteria used are objectively justified. In order to be classified as such they must:

- be appropriate to the tasks carried out;

- correspond to a genuine need of the undertaking.

In *Handels- og Kontorfunktionaerernes Forbund i Danmark v Dansk Arbejdsgiverforening ex p Danfoss* [1989], criteria such as 'flexibility' and 'seniority' could be taken into account in assessing pay. However, there were conditions attached to the ability to invoke 'flexibility'. If it meant that it was an assessment of the employee's work and women received less payment than men, then *prima facie* there would be discrimination and the onus would be on the employer to prove that the difference was objectively justified.

Danfoss is also interesting as it appears to accept 'seniority' as always being a reason to give more pay. This is hard to reconcile with *Nimz*, where it was held that for 'seniority' to be taken into account it would have to be shown that longer experience leads to better performance in the particular job.

SCOPE OF THE DIRECTIVE

The Equal Treatment Directive 76/207 was amended in 2002 by Directive 2002/73 but has now been repealed and replaced by the Equal Treatment Directive 2006/54.

The original Equal Treatment Directive prohibited direct and indirect discrimination on grounds of sex and promoted equal treatment in three employment based areas:

- access to employment and promotion;

- vocational training;

- working conditions.

Similarly Art 14 of the new Equal Treatment Directive provides that there shall be no direct or indirect discrimination on grounds of sex in the public or private sectors, including public bodies in relation to:

- Conditions for access to employment, to self employment or to occupation including selection criteria and recruitment conditions, whatever the branch of activity and at all levels of the professional hierarchy, including promotion.

- Access to all types and to all levels of vocational guidance, vocational training, advanced vocational training and retraining, including practical work experience.

- Employment and working conditions, including dismissals as well as pay as provided for in Article 141 of the EC Treaty (now Art 157 TFEU).

It can be seen that these heads mirror the former law and, therefore, case law decided under the Equal Treatment Directive 76/207 is now considered under the various heads.

Equality of access to employment

This was considered in *Dekker* [1991]. The applicant's offer of employment was withdrawn when the employer discovered that she was pregnant. The employer argued that the intention had not been to discriminate: there had been financial reasons behind the decision, as he would not have recovered the cost of the maternity benefit from the Dutch social fund. Nevertheless, it was held to be a breach of the Directive.

Ellis (1994) 31 CML Rev 43 argues that *Dekker* creates an extension to the idea of direct discrimination. The applicant was not recruited because she was pregnant; since only a woman can become pregnant, her sex was the cause of her failure to get the job. A causation test had been introduced to the concept of direct discrimination. Also, there was no actual male comparator in this case, so it may signal a change of mind on the question of hypothetical comparators after *Macarthys v Smith* [1980].

Despite this criticism, the correctness of *Dekker* [1991] was confirmed in *Mahlburg* [2000]. A heart clinic in Germany refused to take on M, who was pregnant, because of provisions of German law prohibiting the employment of pregnant women in certain circumstances. The clinic took the view that working in an operating theatre would expose M to the harmful effects of substances that pose a risk to health. M successfully challenged her rejection, on the basis that it contravened Directive 76/207. The Court held that 'refusal to employ a woman on account of her pregnancy cannot be justified on grounds relating to the financial loss which an employer . . . would suffer for the duration of her maternity leave. The same conclusion must be drawn as regards the financial loss caused by the fact that the woman appointed cannot be employed in the post concerned for the duration of her pregnancy'.

The case of *Adoulaye v Renault SA* [1999] involved the payment of a lump sum to female workers on commencement of maternity leave. The lump sum was argued to be discriminatory against men, as the birth of a child could have an equal financial impact upon a male employee. The court held that the payment was not discriminatory, as it was designed to offset genuine occupational disadvantages inherent in maternity leave. These disadvantages included missed opportunities for promotion and a lack of knowledge of new technology. The payment was, therefore, accepted as a substantive measure, designed to leave women in the same position as men who were not absent from work.

The borderline between equality of access and conditions of work under the Equal Treatment Directive 76/207 (now replaced by the 2006/54 Directive) and social security under the Social Security Directive 79/7 arose in *Jackson v Chief Adjudication Officer* [1992] and *Meyers v Adjudication Officer* [1995].

In *Jackson*, an income support scheme, the purpose of which was to supplement the income of those with inadequate means of subsistence, could not be brought within the scope of the Equal Treatment directive solely because the method for calculating eligibility could affect a single mother's ability to take up vocational training or employment.

In *Meyers*, a condition for the award of family credit was that the claimant should be engaged in remunerative work. The aim of the benefit was to ensure that families did not find themselves worse off in work than they would have been if not working. It encouraged unemployed people to accept low paid work. Consequently, it was held to be concerned with access to employment.

Equality of access to vocational training

In *Danfoss* [1989], it was held that there was no discrimination where vocational training had been offered to a group of workers who were predominantly male, where there was an objective reason for offering it to them. In this case, it was shown that the vocational training was necessary for the tasks which had been allotted to the predominantly male employees.

Equality of working conditions (including dismissal)

Article 5, Directive 76/207 provided for the application of the equal treatment principle to working conditions and specifically stated that working conditions include dismissal.

This is repeated in Art 14 of the Directive. The cases below were considered under Directive 76/207.

Access to a voluntary redundancy scheme came within the meaning of dismissal for the purposes of Art 5: *Burton v British Railways Board* [1982]. The applicant did not succeed in his claim as, under Art 7(1) of the Social Security Directive, it is possible to exclude from the equal treatment principle the pensionable ages for men and women. Women could apply to the voluntary redundancy scheme at the age of 50, whereas men had to wait until 55. As the ages were linked to the statutory retirement ages for men and women, it was held to be legal.

It was held in *P v S and Cornwall CC* [1996] that that Article prohibited the dismissal of a transsexual for a reason related to gender reassignment. The applicant was dismissed whilst undergoing gender reassignment and claimed to have been the victim of sex discrimination. The CJ applied a purposive interpretation to the Directive. Art 2(1) prohibits discrimination on 'grounds of sex'. The CJ went on to say that this is simply an expression in the relevant field of the principle of equality and that discrimination on grounds of sex was one of the fundamental human rights which the CJ had a duty to ensure. Accordingly, the scope of the Directive could not be confined simply to discrimination based on the fact that a person was of one or other sex. In view of the purpose and the nature of the rights it sought to safeguard, it also applied to discrimination arising from gender reassignment. Where a person was dismissed on the ground of gender reassignment, he or she was to be treated unfavourably by comparison with persons of the sex to which he or she was deemed to belong before undergoing gender reassignment.

Article 7, Directive 76/207 did not apply where retirement age is calculated for 'other purposes', that is, for purposes other than eligibility for State pension: *Marshall v Southampton and South West Hampshire AHA (No 1)* [1984]; *Beets-Proper v Landschot Bankiers* [1986]. In both cases, the applicants had been forced to retire at 60, whereas men could carry on until they were 65. The ages were linked to statutory retirement ages. The CJ held that neither case concerned access to a pension scheme and the Court was, therefore, prepared to draw a distinction between age limits for dismissal (which comes within Art 5) and age limits for pensions (which is caught by the exemption for pensionable ages).

Conditions governing dismissal

The concept that dismissal on grounds of pregnancy is direct discrimination was confirmed in *Brown v Rentokil* [1998]. The defendants had inserted a term into the employment contract that provided that any employee who was absent from work for more than 26 weeks would be dismissed. The applicant became pregnant, was unable to work due to a pregnancy related illness and was dismissed after 26 weeks. The contractual term applied to men and women. It was held that dismissal of a woman during pregnancy on grounds of pregnancy related illness amounted to direct sex discrimination.

By contrast, in *Handels- og Kontorfunktionaerernes Forbund i Danmark (for Hertz) v Dansk Arbejdsgiverforening ex p Aldi Marked K/S* [1990], it was held that the applicant had not been unfairly dismissed for absences from work due to illness caused by a pregnancy two years earlier. The Court said that, after maternity leave, illness due to pregnancy should be treated like any other illness. The question, then, was whether she had suffered adverse treatment compared to a male employee.

Dismissal on grounds of pregnancy was again found to be discriminatory in *Webb v EMO Air Cargo (UK) Ltd* [1994]. The applicant had been employed to replace another employee who was absent on maternity leave. She was found to have been employed for an indefinite period. During the absence of her colleague on maternity leave, the applicant herself became pregnant and was unable to provide cover for the period for which she had been employed. She was then dismissed. It was held that dismissal on grounds of pregnancy of a woman employed for an indefinite period was direct discrimination. Consequently, it was not possible to justify the dismissal on the grounds that she was unable, on a temporary basis, to perform a fundamental condition of her employment contract. The protection could not be made dependent on the question of whether her presence at work during maternity was essential to the proper functioning of the undertaking in which she was employed. A contrary interpretation would render the directive ineffective. It was unclear what the position would have been if the applicant had been employed on a fixed term, as opposed to an indefinite, contract. However, Art 10 of the Pregnancy Directive 92/85 appears to give such workers protection from dismissal during the period of maternity leave.

In *Tele Danmark* [2001], the CJ ruled that the dismissal of any pregnant woman (when the reason for the dismissal is her pregnancy) constitutes direct discrimination – regardless of whether or not she was employed on a fixed term contract. The complainant was recruited by the defendant company for a period of six months in July 1995. In August, she informed the defendant that she was pregnant and expected to give birth in early November. She was dismissed shortly afterwards. The defendant sought to argue that women on fixed term contracts were not protected by Directive 76/207, but the CJ disagreed.

The treatment of pregnancy under equality legislation has been the subject of much criticism. Equality legislation is based on a comparison between the treatment received by a member of one sex compared to a member of the opposite sex. This framework is unsuitable for pregnancy where the needs of the sexes are different. The Pregnancy Directive 92/85 has been welcomed as it breaks away from this comparative analysis and treats pregnancy as a specific issue with special requirements. It introduces minimum protection for three categories of female workers: pregnant workers; workers who have recently given birth; and workers who are breast-feeding. It has not been amended by the Equal Treatment Directive 2006/54.

Its provisions include protection from hazardous substances and protection from dismissal during the period of maternity leave other than in exceptional cases unconnected with pregnancy. It provides for paid time off for ante-natal examinations, minimum requirements for maternity pay, and the protection of part time and fixed term workers during the period of maternity leave.

Adoption leave is not a working condition

In Case 163/82 Commission v Italy [1982], the Commission took enforcement proceedings in respect of an Italian law which provided for eligibility for women but not men for three months compulsory leave after a child under the age of six was adopted into the family. This was held to be legal by the CJ, as it was felt that it was necessary to assimilate conditions of entry of an adopted child into the family to those of a newborn child. The judgment did not follow Advocate General Rozes' opinion. She argued that the paramount aim of adoption leave is to secure the emotional ties between the child and the adoptive family. This is a task which can be performed equally as well by the father as by the mother and, therefore, in the Advocate General's opinion, it is a working condition.

DEROGATIONS FROM THE EQUAL TREATMENT PRINCIPLE

Under the former Equal Treatment Directive 76/207, there were three derogations from the equal treatment principle:

- an occupational qualification provision;

- a pregnancy and maternity provision;

- positive discrimination where it was shown that inequalities actually existed.

Occupational qualification provision

Article 14(2) of the new Equal Treatment Directive 2006/54 maintains the key features of the occupational qualification provision formerly found in Art 2(2) of Directive 76/207.

It provides that Member States may exempt occupational activities for which the sex of the worker constitutes 'a genuine and determining occupational requirement, provided that its objective is legitimate and the requirement is proportionate'.

Certain jobs require physical characteristics which determine that the job can only be done by one sex or the other, for example, actor/actress, model, wet nurse, etc.

Under Art 31(3) of the new Directive, Member States shall assess the occupational activities referred to in Art 14(2) in order to decide, in the light of social developments, whether there is justification for maintaining the exclusions concerned. They are required to notify the Commission of the results of this assessment periodically, but at least every 8 years.

There was a comparable requirement in Art 9(2) of Directive 76/207.

The significance of permitting social considerations to be taken into account is that they vary from State to State. Consequently, there is an element of discretion in the hands of a Member State as to what activities constitute excluded activities for the purpose of Art 31(3) (i.e. the former Art 9(2)).

The scope of this occupational qualification provision was considered in a number of cases under Directive 76/207.

Environment played a crucial part in the outcome of *Johnston v Chief Constable of the Royal Ulster Constabulary* [1986]. The applicant had been refused a renewal of her contract as a member of the RUC full time reserve and was not allowed to attend training in the handling and use of firearms. The reasons given for the refusal were that it was necessary for safeguarding public security and to protect public safety and public order.

The CJ held that regard must be had to the context in which an armed police force carries out its activities, which is determined by the environment. Arming women police officers in Northern Ireland places them under a greater risk of assassination than if they are left unarmed. It was, therefore, contrary to the interests of public safety to provide women officers with arms. On this basis, sex was a determining factor in the carrying out of certain police activities.

The CJ said that, even where a situation came within a derogation, there was an obligation first, under Art 9(2), to periodically assess whether the derogation could still be maintained. Secondly, as this was a derogation from an individual right, the principle of proportionality must be observed. There would have to be a balancing of the interests of equal treatment and public safety and it was for the national court to determine whether an action was proportionate or not.

In *Sirdar v Army Board* [1999], Mrs Sirdar, who had worked as an army chef since 1983, was offered a transfer to the Royal Marines after being made redundant. The offer was withdrawn when it was discovered that Mrs Sirdar was a woman. Army policy prevents women from joining the Royal Marines as every marine is expected to be capable of fighting in a commando unit at short notice. This policy exists because of the small size of Royal Marines units. It was held that the policy of excluding women in this context could be justified proportionally under Art 2(2) of the Equal Treatment Directive.

Ellis (2000) 37 CML Rev 1403 is highly critical of the *Sirdar* judgment. She says, 'the degree of gender-stereotyping . . . is little short of staggering'. *Sirdar* was distinguished soon afterwards in a superficially similar case. In *Kreil v Germany* [2000], Ms K, an electronics expert, applied for a place in the German army to work on the maintenance of electronic weapons systems. However, her application was rejected – the German Constitution prohibited women from being employed in any capacity involving the possible use of arms. (Women were only allowed to serve as medics or musicians.) The CJ held that this prohibition was too general and could not be justified under Art 2(2).

More recently, in *Dory* [2003], both *Sirdar* and *Kreil* were distinguished. The case concerned the requirement in German law that men (but not women) must undergo compulsory military service. The Court held that, while *access to* the military was covered by the Directive, *compulsory* military service was not. This was a matter for the Member States in organising their own internal and external security.

In Case 165/82 *Commission v UK* [1982], the Commission challenged the UK's exclusion under s 6(3) of the Sex Discrimination Act 1975 from the equal treatment principle of employment in a private household or small under-takings where the number of persons does not exceed five. The Commission also challenged the UK's prohibition on men applying for employment or training as midwives. The UK Government argued that the exclusions came within Art 2(2).

The CJ objected to the general nature of the domestic service and small business exceptions. Although there are particular jobs in both sectors which can only be performed by one particular sex, this does not justify exempting them entirely from the equal treatment principle. This was echoed in *Johnston*, where it was again held that a woman could only be excluded from specific activities.

The exclusion relating to midwives was found to be legal. The CJ referred to Art 9(2), Directive 76/207 and the need to constantly review excluded occupational activities in the light of social developments. It was held that the exclusion was appropriate, given personal sensitivities which existed at the date of judgment. These personal sensitivities were capable of making sex a determining factor for the occupational activity. The judgment was contrary to Advocate General Rozes' opinion, who thought that there was nothing in being a midwife itself which justified the exclusion, and laid emphasis on the patient's right to choose the midwife she prefers. The UK has since allowed men to become midwives.

Protection of women, in particular with regard to pregnancy and maternity

Article 2(3) of the former Equal Treatment Directive 76/207 provided for the second exception to the equal treatment principle, whereby provisions were allowed for the protection of women, particularly with regard to pregnancy and maternity.

This exception has been removed and instead Art 15 of the new Equal Treatment Directive provides that a woman on maternity leave shall be entitled, after the end of her period of maternity leave, to return to her job or to an equivalent post on terms and conditions which are no less favourable to her and to benefit from any improvement in working conditions to which she would have been entitled during her absence.

Article 16 contains a similar provision for men returning from paternity leave or for men and women returning from adoption leave.

The Pregnancy Directive 92/85 is not amended by the new Directive 2006/54.

Positive discrimination
Article 2(4) of the earlier Equal Treatment Directive 76/207 provided for positive action for women and permitted measures designed to redress inequality between men and women to promote equal opportunity for men and women and to remove existing inequalities which affected women's opportunities.

It is now dealt with by Art 3 of the new Directive 2006/54, which provides that Member States may maintain or adopt measures within the meaning of Art 157(4) TFEU with a view to ensuring full equality in practice between men and women in working life.

Article 157(4) TFEU provides that, with a view to ensuring full equality in practice between men and women in working life, the principle of equal treatment shall not prevent any Member State from maintaining or adopting measures providing for specific advantages in order to make it easier for the underrepresented sex to pursue a vocational activity or to prevent or compensate for disadvantages in professional careers.

It is believed that although the wording is slightly different from the wording in the Equal Treatment Directive 76/207, the CJ will interpret it in a similar fashion, that is, strictly.

The CJ would only permit positive discrimination where it could be shown that inequalities actually existed.

In *Kalanke v Freie Hansestadt Bremen* [1996], the CJ ruled that national rules which guarantee women absolute and unconditional priority for appointment or promotion, go beyond equal opportunities and exceed the positive action permitted under Art 2(4) Directive 76/207. The Commission has asserted that it makes only rigid quota systems illegal.

A different result was achieved in *Marschall v Land Nordrhein-Westfalen* [1997]. The case concerned a German regional law which provided that, where there were fewer women than men in a higher grade post, women were to be given priority in the event of equal suitability, competence and professional performance unless there were reasons specific to an individual male candidate that tilted matters in his favour. The 'saving clause' led to the CJ holding that the law came within Art 2(4), Directive 76/207 as it allowed for an assessment of individual circumstances.

Both of these rulings were confirmed subsequently. *Kalanke* was followed in *Abrahamsson and Anderson v Fogelqvist* [2000], involving Swedish law conferring priority on female applicants for professorial posts at Swedish universities. This was held to be contrary to the Directive, because there was no saving clause.

Marschall was applied in both *Badeck* [2000] and *Lommers* [2002]. The latter case involved Dutch rules conferring priority on creche places for infants to female employees. Mr L challenged this but the CJ held that it was justifiable. The provision had a similar saving clause to that in *Marschall*, in that fathers could be awarded a creche place for their children in an 'emergency'.

Finally on this point, in *Schnorbus* [2000], the CJ held that Art 2(4) also applies to measures designed to positively discriminate in favour of men. Ms S had applied for a training post with the Ministry of Justice in Hessen, Germany, but had her application deferred because they were oversubscribed. German law conferred priority in such situations on those for whom deferral would constitute 'particular hardship'. One example of hardship was men who may be disadvantaged because of the requirement in German law that men (but not women) must undergo compulsory military service. The Court held that the German rules were acceptable.

The concept of positive discrimination in EU law has been extended by its inclusion in the agreement annexed to the Social Protocol of the Treaty on European Union. Article 6(3) allows for measures of positive discrimination.

EFFECTIVE REMEDIES

Starting with the cases of *Von Colson and Kamman v Land Nordrhein-Westfalen* [1984] and *Harz v Deutsche Tradaz* [1984], it can be seen that the Directive requires real and effective sanctions where there has been a breach of the equal treatment principle. Although there is no express provision to this effect in the Directive, Art 6, Directive 76/207 requires the Member States to introduce measures so that applicants who feel wronged by the failure to apply the equal treatment to them can pursue their claims by judicial process. From this, the CJ has adduced the need for effective sanctions, and said in its judgment in *Von Colson* that 'it is impossible to establish real equality of opportunity without an appropriate system of sanctions'.

The principle was applied in relation to British legislation in *Marshall v Southampton and South West Hampshire AHA (No 2)* [1993]. An arbitrary upper limit of £6,250 compensation in the Sex Discrimination Act 1975 for the victim of discrimination was held to be contrary to Art 6 of the Equal Treatment Directive. The CJ held that, where financial compensation is the method of fulfilling the Directive's objectives, it must enable the financial loss and damage actually suffered to be made good. In this respect, the judgment differed from Advocate General Gerven's opinion, which had stated that although the damages must be 'adequate' they did not have to be equal to the damage suffered. The court also said that an award of damages could not leave out matters such as 'effluxion of time' which might reduce the value of the award, and, therefore, interest was payable on the damages. Finally, it was also held that for limited purposes Art 6 had direct effect. Where a Member State has been free to choose from amongst a number of solutions which are suitable for achieving the objective of the directive and has made its choice, then Art 6 may be relied on.

EQUAL TREATMENT DIRECTIVE 2006/54 – TITLE III

In Title III of the new Directive, there are now provisions relating to equality bodies, remedies, compliance, etc. which bring this sex equality secondary legislation into line with other anti-discriminatory directives (e.g. covering race, disability, etc).

FURTHER SECONDARY LEGISLATION

For further legislation on equality see:

- Council Directive 2000/43/EC of 29 June 2000 implementing the principle of equal treatment between persons irrespective of racial or ethnic origin, which implements the principle of equal treatment in employment and training irrespective of religion or belief, disability, age or sexual orientation in employment, training and membership and involvement in organisations of workers and employers.

- See also Directive 79/7/EEC dealing with equal treatment in state social security; Directive 2004/113 dealing with equal treatment in access to and supply of goods and services; the Pregnant Workers Directive 92/85/EC dealing with issues concerning health and safety at work; and the Parental Leave Directive 96/37/EC on the framework agreement on parental leave.

- See also Directive 2008/104/EC of the European Parliament and the Council of 19 November 2008 on temporary agency work. The purpose of this Directive is to ensure the protection of temporary agency workers and to improve the quality of temporary agency work by ensuring that the principle of equal treatment is applied to temporary agency workers, and by recognising temporary work agencies as employers.

You should now be confident that you would be able to tick all of the boxes on the checklist at the beginning of this chapter. To check your knowledge of EU sex equality legislation why not visit the companion website and take the Multiple Choice Question test. Check your understanding of the terms and vocabulary used in this chapter with the flashcard glossary.

7

Free movement of goods

Recognise the different ways in which the free movement of goods can be hindered by tariff and non-tariff barriers to trade ☐

Distinguish between customs duties and charges having equivalent effect and explain how they are regulated by the TFEU (formerly EC Treaty) ☐

Distinguish between a charge having an equivalent effect to a customs duty and a discriminatory tax ☐

Explain the scope of Article 110 TFEU (formerly Art 90 TEC) and how it is applied to discriminatory taxes ☐

Distinguish between quantitative restrictions and measures having equivalent effect ☐

Distinguish between distinctly and indistinctly applicable rules ☐

Discuss the rule of reason introduced in *Cassis de Dijon* ☐

Explain the decision in *Keck and Mithouard* ☐

Explain when a Member State may rely on the Art 36 TFEU (formerly Art 30 TEC) derogations ☐

INTRODUCTION

The free movement of goods is possibly the central aspect of the EU's internal market. The principle of free movement of goods is achieved by three separate means:

Tariff Barriers to Trade

1   Prohibition of customs duties and charges having an equivalent effect on goods from other Member States – Arts 28 and 30 TFEU (formerly Arts 23 and 25 TEC).

2   Prohibition of discriminatory taxation on goods from other Member States – Art 110 TFEU (formerly Art 90 TEC).

Non-Tariff Barriers to Trade

3   Prohibition of quantitative restrictions and measures having an equivalent effect on imports and exports between Member States – Arts 34, 35 and 36 TFEU (formerly Arts 28, 29 and 30 TEC).

Before looking at these in depth, it is helpful to understand what 'goods' means under EU law. 'Goods' are defined very widely. According to the Court of Justice in *Commission v Italy* [1968]:

> By 'goods' ... there must be understood products which can be valued in money, and which are capable, as such, of forming the subject of commercial transactions.

Thus, anything which can be bought or sold is 'goods'. In *Commission v Belgium* [1992], the CJ rejected an argument put forward by Belgium that waste could not be 'goods'. Anything shipped across a border for the purposes of commercial transactions was covered.

The free movement provisions apply equally to goods manufactured or produced in the EU and to those in free circulation there, regardless of their country of origin (*Donckerwolcke* [1976]).

TARIFF BARRIERS TO TRADE

CUSTOMS UNION

According to Art 28 TFEU (formerly Art 23 TEC), 'the Union shall be based upon a customs union which shall cover all trade in goods and which shall involve the prohibition between Member States of customs duties on imports and exports and of all charges having equivalent effect, and the adoption of a common customs tariff in their relations with third countries'. Art 28 TFEU is directly effective (*Van Gend en Loos* [1963]).

Article 28 TFEU, therefore, creates the Customs Union. It has two parts:

1   common customs tariff;
2   prohibition on customs duties between Member States.

COMMON CUSTOMS TARIFF (CCT)

The CCT applies to all goods imported into the EU from countries such as Japan and the USA. The Commission sets the level of the tariff for each product. This led to a threatened trade war with the United States in the early months of 1999, as the Commission had set a lower tariff for bananas imported from former British colonies in the West Indies than for bananas imported from Central and South American countries, where many US-controlled banana plantations are based. The tariffs collected by each State's customs authorities are paid into the EU's central budget.

PROHIBITION OF CUSTOMS DUTIES BETWEEN MEMBER STATES

Article 28 TFEU (formerly Art 23 TEC) states that the Customs Union involves a prohibition on 'Customs duties on imports or exports' and 'charges having equivalent effect' between Member States. This prevents Member States from charging importers for bringing goods into that State from another Member State, whether the goods were produced in the EU or not.

Article 30 TFEU (formerly Art 25 TEC) (described as the 'standstill' provision) prohibits the introduction between Member States of any new customs duties on imports or exports or any charges having equivalent effect.

What are 'customs duties' and 'charges having equivalent effect'?

A customs duty is any charge that is imposed on goods because they are imported (*Steinike & Weinleg* [1977]). Article 28 TFEU prohibits these charges because they may have the effect of reducing imports, and hence trade, by making imported goods more expensive. A simple prohibition on customs duties would have allowed customs authorities to continue to charge importers through less obvious means. Hence Art 28 TFEU also prohibits charges having 'equivalent effect' to customs duties. The meaning of the term 'charges having an equivalent effect to a customs duty' was laid down by the CJ in *Commission v Italy (Statistical Levy case)* [1969] as:

> Any pecuniary charge, whatever its size and name, imposed on any goods by reason of the fact that they cross a frontier, and which is not a customs duty in the strict sense, is a 'charge having equivalent effect' (*Commission v Italy* [1969]).

Many customs duties are imposed to make imports relatively more expensive and hence protect domestic production. But there is no requirement that the charge be levied for protectionist reasons. There may even be no domestic market in need of protection; but this will not stop the charge from infringing Art 28 TFEU (formerly Art 23 TEC). In *Sociaal Fonds voor de Diamantarbeiders* [1969], a charge of 1/3 per cent was imposed on unworked diamonds imported into Belgium. The purpose was to raise funds for workers in the diamond-mining industry in Africa. Various importers of industrial diamonds challenged the charge. Following a reference from the Belgian court, the CJ held that the charge contravened Art 28 TFEU.

When a breach of Art 28 TFEU is established after duties or equivalent charges have been paid, then the Member State in question is, in principle, obliged to repay the importer/exporter, as the case may be (*San Giorgio* [1983]; *Dilexport* [1999]). Moreover, national rules of evidence which have the effect of making it virtually impossible or excessively difficult to secure repayment of duties or equivalent charges levied in breach of Art 28 TFEU are incompatible with EU law (*San Giorgio*). However, EU law does not require the repayment of the duty or equivalent charge in circumstances where this would unjustly enrich the person concerned (*Just* [1980]). This would occur in a situation, for example, where the burden of the charge has been transferred in whole or in part to other persons. Thus, if an importer had paid the duty or equivalent charge, but then passed on the cost to the distributor of the goods in the importing State, to order repayment to the importer would over-compensate them (*Société Comateb & Others* [1997]).

What if the charges are for services carried out for the benefit of the importer?

A charge for services imposed in the general interest under national law (e.g. health inspections or quality control), is nevertheless in breach of Art 28 TFEU (formerly Art 23 TEC) (*Rewe-Zentralfinanz* [1973]).

A charge which is imposed for services provided to the importer/exporter by the customs authorities (e.g. warehouse facilities) may be compatible with Art 28 TFEU (formerly Art 23 TEC), provided that the services give a 'tangible benefit' to the importer/exporter, and the charge does not exceed the cost of the service. In *Donner* [1983], the Dutch Post Office charged Andreas Donner a fee for dealing with the payment of VAT on a number of books he had imported into the Netherlands. This was held by the CJ to be capable of being regarded as payment for services and, therefore, permissible.

What if charges are for services imposed under EU law?

Where the services charged for are imposed under EU law, then a charge could be regarded as a payment for services and, therefore, it would be permissible for the State to require payment of it (*Bauhuis* [1977]). Where the State is permitted to charge for services, it is only entitled to recover the actual cost of the service, and no more (*Denkavit* [1982]).

PROHIBITION OF DISCRIMINATORY TAXATION: ART 110 TFEU (FORMERLY ART 90 TEC)

No Member State shall impose, directly or indirectly, on the products of the other Member States any internal taxation of any kind in excess of that imposed directly or indirectly on similar domestic products. Furthermore, no Member State shall impose on the products of other Member States any internal taxation of such nature as to afford indirect protection to other products.

Article 110 TFEU allows Member States the freedom to establish their own taxation system (often referred to as 'excise duties' in the UK) for any given product, provided there is no discrimination against imports, or indirect protection of domestic products. This can lead to significant differences in prices of the same goods from one Member State to another. For example, in the UK, the most heavily taxed goods are cigarettes, alcohol, perfume and petrol. Because cigarettes and alcohol are taxed at a much lower rate in France, the phenomenon of the 'booze cruise' – whereby UK nationals take the ferry across the English Channel to France in order to buy those goods relatively cheaply – was created. Of course, under UK law – the Customs & Excise Management Act 1979 – individuals are not permitted to bring into the UK an unlimited amount of alcohol and cigarettes. HM Customs & Excise officers have to be vigilant in order to catch people bringing back consignments of those goods which are for commercial purposes, as opposed to personal use. Anyone bringing in goods for commercial purposes without payment of excise duty is potentially liable to have the goods forfeited – and to have their vehicle forfeited too. However, forfeiture of property in this way has been held to be a potential breach of both the free movement of goods under Art 34 TFEU (formerly 28 TEC) and Art 1 of the First protocol of the European Convention of Human Rights (the right to property). Several cases in this area are discussed in Andrew Lidbetter's article, 'Customs, cars and Article 1 of the First protocol' (2004) 3 EHRLR 272.

'Tax'

The borderline between 'customs duties' (considered above) and 'taxes' may be difficult to draw. However, the CJ has stated that Arts 28 and 110 TFEU (formerly Arts 23 and 90 TEC) are mutually exclusive, so it is important to make the distinction clear. This is especially so given that many 'customs duties' are disguised as 'taxes'. A 'tax' was defined in *Commission v France* [1981] as one that related to:

> A general system of internal duties applied systematically to categories of products in accordance with objective criteria irrespective of the origin of the products.

'Products of the other Member States'

Despite the clear implication of this phrase, the CJ has held that the prohibition of discriminatory taxation must apply to goods manufactured or produced *outside* the EU, but which are in free circulation inside it (*Coopera-tiva Co-Frutta* [1987]).

Article 110(1) TFEU: discrimination between imports and 'similar domestic products'

The CJ had held that Art 110(1) TFEU must be construed broadly (*Commission v France* [1980]). It is not necessary that the imported and domestic products in question are *identical*. They need only be 'similar'. The test is whether the products 'have similar characteristics and meet the same needs from the point of view of consumers . . . not according to whether they are strictly identical but whether their use is similar or comparable' (*Commission v Denmark* [1986]).

Most cases have arisen in the context of alcoholic drinks. In *John Walker & Sons* [1986], where different rates of tax were imposed by Denmark on fruit liqueur wines and whisky, the CJ held that it was not enough for 'similarity' that both products contained alcohol. To be 'similar', the alcohol would have to be present in more or less equal measure. As whisky contained twice as much alcohol as fruit liqueur wines (40 per cent to 20 per cent), they were not similar products for the purposes of Art 110(1) TFEU.

In *Commission v France* [1980], under French legislation, grain-based spirits (such as whisky and gin, which were largely imported) were subject to a much higher tax regime than fruit-based spirits (such as cognac and brandy), of which there was heavy French production. The European Commission, arguing that *all* spirits were 'similar', alleged a breach of Art 110(1) TFEU. The French government argued that a distinction should be drawn between two classes of spirits: aperitifs and digestives. The former (including whisky and gin) were drunk, usually diluted with water or a mixer, before meals. The latter (including cognac and brandy) were beverages consumed, neat, at the end of a meal. Hence the two types were not 'similar'. The Court rejected this distinction. All the drinks could be consumed before, during or after meals or at any other time. The Court also rejected any distinction based on flavour. Although there were undoubtedly 'shades of difference' in the flavour of the various drinks, this criterion was 'too variable in time and space to supply by itself a sufficiently sound basis for distinction'. In the end, the Court concluded that it did not need to decide whether the drinks were 'similar' because it was 'impossible reasonably to contest that without exception they are in at least partial competition', and hence Art 110(2) TFEU applied instead.

Where a system of taxation is *prima facie* non-discriminatory, but in effect discriminates against the imported product, it will still amount to a breach of Art 110(1) TFEU. In *Humblot* [1985], the French government applied road tax on a sliding scale, with a significantly higher rate payable on cars exceeding 16 cv. No cars exceeding such capacity were made in France. H, a French taxpayer who imported a 36 cv Mercedes from Germany, sought repayment through the French courts of the excess tax. The CJ held that such a system of taxation amounted to 'indirect' discrimination based on nationality, contrary to Art 110(1) TFEU.

Where a Member State applies a tax in accordance with criteria which indirectly discriminates against imports, it may be possible for the tax to be objectively justified. In *Commission v France (Sweet Wines case)* [1987], France taxed sweet wines produced in a traditional manner at a lower rate than liqueur wines. It was held by the Court that this amounted to indirect discrimination, but the tax could be objectively justified. Sweet wines were generally made in areas with poor soil and low rainfall and where the local economy was largely dependent on wine production.

Article 110(2) TFEU: indirect protection of domestic products

For the purposes of Art 110(2) TFEU, it is not even necessary for the products in question to be similar. Instead, it applies to 'all forms of indirect tax protection in the case of products which, without being similar within the meaning of Art 90(1) TEC, are nevertheless in competition, even partial, indirect or potential competition with each other' (*Cooperativa Co-Frutta* [1987]). It is, thus, much wider in scope than Art 110(1) TFEU. Frequently, cases will be argued under Art 110(1) TFEU first. If the Court is not satisfied that the products are 'similar', it will then consider whether they are in competition.

Commission v UK [1983] concerned excise duties imposed on beer and wine in the UK in the late 1970s. Wine was being taxed at £3.25 per gallon, while beer was being taxed at only 61p per gallon. The vast majority of wine consumed in the UK was imported (from France, Germany and Italy), while beer was predominantly domestically produced. The Commission alleged that the tax differential amounted to discrimination against imports. The UK claimed that the products, although both alcoholic drinks, were not 'similar'. The CJ agreed that 'in view of the substantial differences between wine and beer' in terms of their different manufacturing processes and natural properties, the products were not 'similar'. There was, therefore, no breach of Art 110(1) TFEU. However, the Court went on to hold that the UK was in breach of Art 110(2) TFEU. The Court found that the effect of subjecting wine to a higher level of tax afforded protection to domestic beer production. The effect of the UK tax system was to 'stamp wine with the hallmarks of a luxury product which, in view of the tax burden which it bears, can scarcely constitute, in the eyes of the consumer, a genuine alternative to the typical domestically produced beverage'.

Cooperativa Co-Frutta [1987] is an example of the latter approach. A consumer tax was imposed in Italy on both domestic and imported bananas. As the domestic production was tiny, this in effect amounted to a tax on imports. No such charges were placed on other fresh fruit, such as pears, which were principally home-produced. The CJ found this to be indirect protection of domestic fruit production, and contrary to Art 110(2) TFEU.

Finally, it should be noted that if there is found to be a protective effect in breach of Art 110(2) TFEU, then the national legislation must be amended to remove the protective effect. However, provided this is achieved, it is not necessary for the rates of tax on the different but competing products to be equalised.

CHECKLIST FOR APPLICATION OF ARTS 30 AND 110 TFEU (FORMERLY ARTS 25 AND 90 TEC)

Is the tariff a customs duty or charge having an equivalent effect? If so, apply Art 30 TFEU (formerly Art 25 TEC).

Is the tariff an internal tax? If so, apply Art 110 TFEU (formerly Art 90 TEC).

Art 110(1) TFEU applies to 'similar' goods. If the import and the domestic product are 'similar', the tax burden must be the same. Both direct and indirect discrimination must be removed by the Member State. Indirect discrimination may be objectively justified subject to the principle of proportionality.

If the imported and domestic goods are not similar, but compete with one another, Art 110(2) TFEU requires any protective effect conferred on the domestic product to be removed.

NON-TARIFF BARRIERS TO TRADE

PROHIBITION OF QUANTITATIVE RESTRICTIONS ON IMPORTS AND EXPORTS AND MEASURES HAVING EQUIVALENT EFFECT: ARTS 34, 35 AND 36 TFEU (FORMERLY ARTS 28, 29 AND 30 TEC)

A simple abolition of customs duties under Art 28 TFEU (formerly Art 23 TEC) would not have been sufficient to guarantee the free movement of goods. There are an infinite variety of legal, administrative and procedural practices that may be adopted by Member States that have the *effect* of reducing intra-Community trade. Arts 34 and 35 TFEU (formerly Arts 28 and 29 TEC) are designed to eliminate these practices. Art 36 TFEU (formerly Art 30 TEC) lays down six grounds on which a Member State can justify the hindrance of intra-EU trade subject to the principle of proportionality.

ARTICLE 35 TFEU (FORMERLY ARTICLE 29 TEC)

Article 35 TFEU (formerly Article 29 TEC) provides that 'Quantitative restrictions on exports, and all measures having equivalent effect, shall be prohibited between Member States'. Under Art 35 TFEU the *Dassonville* formula does not apply. In order to breach Art 35 TFEU, national laws must be protectionist, that is, national laws must have the restriction of exports as their specific object or effect. This was established in *Groenveld* [1979]. Dutch law banned the possession of horsemeat by the manufacturers of meat products. When one such manufacturer brought a challenge to the Dutch rules alleging a breach of Art 35 TFEU, the CJ held there had been no breach, because the law drew no distinction between meat products destined for the Dutch market and those intended for export.

Conversely, in *Bouhelier* [1977], French law imposed a licensing system on certain watches – but only those intended for export. The CJ held that this did constitute a breach of Art 35 TFEU. Similarly, in *R v Thompson* [1978], where UK law banned the exportation of silver coins, and in *Dusseldorp* [1998], where Dutch law restricted the exportation of certain waste products for recycling, both were held to constitute a breach of Art 35 TFEU.

It has long been assumed that equally applicable rules were not within Art 35 TFEU as a result of comments in *Groenveld* and the results in that case. As a consequence of *Gybrechts* [2008], it is now clear that even an equally applicable rule may, as a matter of fact, disadvantage exports relative to domestic sales, contrary to Art 35 TFEU. The case concerned a rule which applied without distinction between domestic sale and exports yet which the court nevertheless found to be within Art 35 TFEU (see A Dawes, 'A Freedom Reborn? The New Yet Unclear Scope of Article 29', (2009) 34 *ELRev* 639).

ARTICLE 34 TFEU (FORMERLY ARTICLE 28 TEC)

Article 34 TFEU (formerly Article 28 TEC) provides that 'Quantitative restrictions on imports and all measures having equivalent effect shall ... be prohibited between Member States'. (Art 35 TFEU provides the same for exports.) A national law or measure that infringes Art 34 TFEU is *prima facie* contrary to EU law; however, Art 36 provides that Art 34 TFEU will not apply to certain restrictions which are justifiable on various grounds. In addition to these derogations, the CJ has developed its own line of case law, in which it has held that certain measures will not breach Art 34 TFEU if they are necessary to satisfy mandatory requirements (i.e. national rules which may be raised by Member States as justification for overriding Art 34). This is known as the 'rule of reason', and was introduced in *Cassis de Dijon* [1979]. In addition, the CJ introduced the principle of mutual recognition, namely that goods which have been lawfully marketed in one Member State should be able to move freely in other Member States.

Further, as will be seen below in *Keck and Mithouard* [1993], the CJ has confirmed that national laws which relate to 'Selling Arrangements' are outside the scope of Art 34 TFEU altogether, provided that the national rules in question apply equally to all traders in law and in fact.

All of these aspects of EU law on the free movement of goods will be considered in detail below.

Although Art 34 TFEU is directly effective, it is important to note that it is addressed to, and only relates to measures taken by, or on behalf of, the Member States. 'State' has, however, been given a very wide meaning. It includes, for example:

- national and local government, in its many forms;

- semi-public bodies such as quangos (e.g. *Apple & Pear Development Council v KJ Lewis Ltd* [1983]);

■ the post office (*Commission v France* [1985]);

■ the police force (*R v Chief Constable of Sussex ex p International Traders' Ferry Ltd* [1998], House of Lords).

In *R v Pharmaceutical Society of GB ex p Association of Pharmaceutical Importers* [1989] the CJ held that rules established by regulatory agencies and professional bodies established under statutory authority may also be subject to the control of EU law.

In *Commission v France (French Farmers case)* [1997], the CJ held that Art 34 TFEU (formerly Art 28 TEC) in conjunction with former Art 10 TEC can apply to Member States even though the hindrance of trade may have been due to the actions of private parties. In this case, French farmers had blocked imports of strawberries coming into France from Spain. The Commission brought an Art 258 TFEU (formerly Art 226 TEC) action against France for failing to take sufficient measures to ensure that the right to free movement of goods was protected.

> ▶ COMMISSION v FRANCE (French Farmers case) [1997]
>
> **French farmers disrupted imports of strawberries coming into France from Spain. The Commission brought an Art 258 TFEU (formerly Art 226 TEC) action against France for failing to secure the free movement of goods.**
>
> **The CJ held that Art 34 TFEU (formerly Art 28 TEC), together with former Art 10 TEC, imposed on Member States an obligation to take all the appropriate measures necessary to protect the free movement of goods within their own territory.**

In *Schmidberger v Austria* [2003], the CJ held that Austria had infringed both Arts 34 and 35 TFEU (formerly Arts 28 and 29 TEC), combined with Art 4 TEU (formerly Art 10 TEC), for failing to stop a demonstration by an environmental group which led to the closure for almost 30 hours of the Brenner motorway, a major transit route between northern Europe and the north of Italy. However, the CJ did accept that the infringement was objectively justified (see below).

'Quantitative restrictions'

A 'quantitative restriction' has been defined as any measure which amounts to a total, or partial, restraint on imports, exports or goods in transit (*Riseria Luigi Geddo v Ente Nazionale Risi* [1973]). This most obviously includes a quota system (*Salgoil* [1968]), but also includes an outright ban on imports (*Commission v Italy* [1961]; *R v Henn and Darby* [1979]).

'Measures having equivalent effect' to quantitative restrictions (MEQR)

The classic formulation of what is meant by MEQR was given by the CJ in *Dassonville* [1974]:

> All trading rules enacted by Member States which are capable of hindering, directly or indirectly, actually or potentially, intra-Community trade are to be considered as measures having an effect equivalent to quantitative restrictions.

This has become known as the *Dassonville* 'formula'. The definition given to 'measures having an effect equivalent to quantitative restrictions' is very wide and means that virtually any measure which limits imports or exports in any way could be caught by Art 34 TFEU. There is no requirement of discrimination. The term 'all trading rules' in *Dassonville* have in some following judgements been replaced by broader terms, such as 'all rules' or 'all measures' (e.g. *Commission v Spain* [2009] and *Commission v Germany* [2007]).

Examples of MEQRs

The following is a list of examples of national laws that have been held to be prohibited by Art 34 TFEU. This is *not* a comprehensive list. Remember that many of these laws are capable of justification under either Art 36 TFEU or the *Cassis de Dijon* principle.

- A classic method adopted by Member States to introduce import restrictions is to insist on importers being licensed *Commission v Finland* [2007]. These are often held to be justified on health grounds. Nevertheless, the CJ has consistently held that such requirements are *prima facie* in breach of Art 34 TFEU. The reasons are twofold: first, because applying for licences is a time-consuming process, importers will be unable to import goods while awaiting their licence; secondly, some importers may be disinclined to go to the trouble of applying for a licence. If even one potential importer decides not to apply for a licence, then there has been a restriction on imports. One such case, *Commission v UK* [1983], will be considered below.

■ National rules requiring goods to be marked with their country of origin could also infringe Art 34 TFEU because that would impose extra burdens on importers, many of whom would not necessarily be aware of the national law and so face difficulties in complying with it. In *Dassonville* itself, D was a trader in Belgium who imported a consignment of Johnnie Walker and Vat 69 Scotch whisky from France. Under Belgian law, a certificate of origin was required for all imports of a range of goods, including Scotch whisky. France had no such legislation and the French distributor was unable to provide a certificate of origin, which could only be issued by the UK customs authorities. Despite this, D went ahead with the transaction, using forged documents. The Belgian authorities discovered the forgery and D was prosecuted. He pleaded Art 34 TFEU in his defence, and the Belgian court referred the matter to the CJ, which found that the Belgian law infringed Art 34.

▶ DASSONVILLE [1974]

Under Belgian law, a certificate of origin was required for Scotch whisky. This could only be issued by UK customs. *Dassonville* imported Scotch whisky into Belgium through France and forged a certificate of origin. When he was prosecuted he pleaded that the requirement for such a certificate constituted a MEQR and was, therefore, prohibited under Art 34 TFEU.

The CJ held that the requirement did constitute a MEQR, which it described as 'all trading rules enacted by Member States which are capable of hindering, directly or indirectly, actually or potentially, intra-[EU] trade'.

■ Government-sponsored campaigns to encourage consumers to buy domestic products clearly infringe Art 34 TFEU. This is because they have the potential (at least) to influence traders and shoppers into discriminating against imports and thus frustrating free movement. In *Commission v*

Ireland [1982], the Irish Goods Council was a semi-public body given the task by the Irish Government of promoting Irish goods on the basis of their Irish origin. The Council was given financial support to launch a major advertising campaign by the Irish Ministry of Industry. The activities of the Council were held to have infringed Art 34 TFEU.

■ However, *Commission v Ireland* was distinguished in *Apple & Pear Development Council v KJ Lewis Ltd* [1983]. The Council had been set up to promote the consumption of apples and pears grown in England and Wales *via* a television advertising campaign (using the slogan 'Polish up your English') and research projects. Several growers refused to pay the levy due, and were sued by the Council. In their defence they argued Art 34 TFEU. The CJ held that it was permissible to promote a national product by reference to its particular qualities, but not simply because it was from a particular State. The EU's internal market rules encourage competition based on quality, but not nationality.

■ National laws which relate to how products are packaged may well infringe Art 34 TFEU, because they increase the costs of manufacturers in other Member States, who may have to develop special packaging processes purely for the importing State. It may also inhibit distributors and retailers in that State from importing goods that do not comply with the national law. Conversely, it will be much easier for domestic manufacturers to comply with their own national requirements as to packaging. In *Walter Rau v De Smedt* [1982], Belgian law prohibited the sale of margarine otherwise than in cubes, ostensibly to help consumers distinguish such products from butter. Rau, a German company, contracted to supply De Smedt, a Belgian supermarket chain, with 15,000 kg of margarine. When the margarine was delivered it was in truncated cone-shaped containers. De Smedt, aware of the requirements of Belgian law, refused to accept delivery. Rau sued for specific performance of the contract. On a reference to the CJ, the Court ruled that the Belgian law was a measure equivalent to a quantitative restriction and, therefore, infringed Art 34 TFEU.

■ There are other cases that deal with rules concerning the use of goods. In *Commission v Portugal* [2008] a Portuguese measure was challenged which prohibited sticking tinted plastic onto car windows to turn them into tinted windows. The case *Åklagaren v Percy Mickelsson and Joakim Roos* [2009] concerned the governmental prohibition of the use of jet-skis except on designated waterways, but the government did not designate any waterways. In *Commission v Italy* [2009] Italian rules were challenged as they prohibited the towing of trailer behind a motorcycle. In these use cases the court ruled that even though there is no outright prohibition of the importation or sale of a product these measures indirectly achieved the same effect and, therefore, these measures constitute MEQRs. The court treated market access as an extension of equal treatment. In *Alfa Vita* [2006] the court went even further when it applied Art 34 to measures which did not prevent sales but merely diminished them; it merely inhibits sales by imposing a cost burden. It was not necessary to show unequal effect to engage Art 34 TFEU.

NON-DISCRIMINATORY NATIONAL RULES: THE PRINCIPLE OF MUTUAL RECOGNITION AND THE 'RULE OF REASON'

The wide scope of the *Dassonville* formula (see above) was confirmed by the CJ in its *Cassis de Dijon* decision [1979]. Art 34 TFEU can catch both distinctly and non-distinctly applicable measures:

> **Distinctly applicable measures** – apply to imports only and may be discriminatory.
>
> **Indistinctly applicable measures** – apply to both imports and domestically produced goods and may be indirectly discriminatory or non-discriminatory.

The CJ recognised that Member States may have introduced indistinctly applicable rules for legitimate reasons, such as consumer protection. Should these rules also be caught by Art 34 TFEU? The CJ sought to address this issue in its *Cassis de Dijon* decision.

In *Cassis*, Rewe-Zentrale, a firm of German importers, wanted to import a French blackcurrant liqueur (called 'cassis') with an alcohol content of about 15–20 per cent proof. They applied to the German authorities for permission but were informed that the French cassis was of insufficient alcohol strength. German law laid down a minimum alcohol level of 25 per cent per litre of cassis. When Rewe challenged the German law, the case was referred to the CJ for a preliminary ruling, giving the Court the opportunity to introduce the 'rule of reason' and the principle of mutual recognition.

The Court began by quoting *Dassonville*, but added that in the absence of Community rules harmonising the production and marketing of alcohol, it is for the Member States themselves to regulate these matters in their own territory. It added that:

> Obstacles to movement within the Union resulting from disparities between the national laws relating to the marketing of the products in question must be accepted in so far as these provisions may be recognised as being necessary in order to satisfy mandatory requirements relating in particular to the effectiveness of fiscal supervision, the protection of public health, the fairness of commercial transactions and the defence of the consumer.

Prior to *Cassis*, national laws that were found to be in breach of Art 34 TFEU, as defined in *Dassonville*, could only be justified under Art 34 TFEU. After *Cassis*, national laws could be saved either by the 'rule of reason' or by Art 34 TFEU. Initially, the CJ stated that *Cassis* only operated to save those national laws that apply 'without discrimination' to domestic and imported products (*Gilli & Andres* [1980]) and that discriminatory national laws may only be saved by using Art 36 TFEU. However, in more recent case law, the CJ has accepted justification of distinctly applicable/directly discriminatory measures on the ground of environmental protection, one of the mandatory requirements (*Commission v Belgium (Walloon Waste)* [1992]; *Preussen Elektra* [2001]). This has led to confusion in the case law and there have been calls by Shaw, Hunt & Wallace (*Economic and Social Law of the European Union*, Palgrave Macmillan, Basingstoke (2007)), for the derogations set out in Art 36 TFEU over fifty years ago to be reformed.

'The rule of reason': the mandatory requirements

In its *Cassis de Dijon* judgment, the CJ referred to four 'mandatory requirements', that is, national rules which may be relied upon by Member States as justification for overriding Art 34 TFEU if there is a very good reason for doing so. These are:

- effectiveness of fiscal supervision;
- protection of public health;
- fairness of commercial transactions;
- defence of the consumer.

In *Prantl* [1984], P was prosecuted under German unfair competition law for importing Italian wine in bottles, which were very similar in shape and design to distinctively-shaped German bottles protected under German law as designating a particular quality wine. In his defence, P argued that the German law infringed Art 34 TFEU; the German authorities tried to claim that the law was justified in the interests of fair trading. The CJ held that as the bottles were fairly and traditionally manufactured in Italy, there was no justification for excluding them from Germany.

In *Cassis de Dijon*, the Court listed four grounds 'in particular', implying that its list was not closed. Indeed, the grounds given in *Cassis* (see above) have since been added to in subsequent case law. In *Criminal Proceedings Against Bellamy and English Shop Wholesale* [2001] the Court ruled that measures having equivalent effect are prohibited by Art 34 TFEU unless their application can be justified by a 'public-interest objective'. Some examples of 'public-interest' are listed below:

- Protection of cultural and socio-cultural characteristics

In *Cinéthèque* [1985], French legislation prohibited the marketing of videos within 12 months of first being shown at the cinema. C, a French video distributor, had acquired the rights to distribute a video in October 1983. However, the film had only been released at the French cinema in June. C challenged the law and the case was referred to the CJ, which accepted that the restriction was justified, and that the law was not in breach of Art 34 TFEU. The Court referred to the 'protection of the cinema as a means of cultural expression, of which protection was necessary in view of the rapid development of other modes of film distribution'.

- Protection of the environment

In *Commission v Denmark* [1988], the CJ accepted that environmental protection was another mandatory requirement. Danish legislation required that all beer and soft drinks sold in Denmark had to be packaged in re-usable containers. The European Commission challenged the legislation, alleging breach of Art 34 TFEU; the CJ ruled that it was justifiable. In the event, the Court decided that the Danish legislation was unjustified, applying the proportionality test, that is, there were other means available to the Danish that would also protect the environment but in a way that was less restrictive on intra-State trade. In *Radlberger Getränkegesellschaft mbH & Co v Land Baden-Württemberg* [2004] the Court had to deal with non-recyclable packaging and return systems. It accepted rules which would not only have significant effect on trade but probably on importers much more than on domestic producers, because those rules did serve an important environmental goal.

Maintenance of press diversity

In *Familapress* [1997], Austrian legislation prohibited newspapers and magazines from incorporating crossword puzzles with cash prizes. This was designed to help smaller publishers compete against much larger publishers who would otherwise be able to attract bigger readerships by offering bigger cash prizes and thus maintain a diverse press. As German law contained no such prohibition, this Austrian law prevented German publishers who published magazines with prize competitions in them from selling their magazines in Austria. The CJ held that the Austrian law was justifiable and introduced the maintenance of press diversity as a new mandatory requirement.

Socio-cultural characteristics

In *Torfaen BC v B&Q plc*, B&Q had been prosecuted for opening its shops on Sundays in breach of UK law. In its defence, B&Q argued that the ban on trading on Sundays (save for certain goods) was in breach of Art 34 TFEU (formerly Art 28 TEC), since the effect of the law was to reduce its total turnover by 10 per cent with a corresponding reduction in the number of sales of imports. On a reference from the UK court, the CJ accepted that *prima facie*, the national law fell within the scope of Art 34 TFEU (formerly Art 28 TEC) as defined in *Dassonville*. Nevertheless, it held that the national rules governing the opening hours of retail premises 'reflect certain political and economic choices in so far as their purpose is to ensure that working and non-working hours are so arranged as to accord with national or regional socio-cultural characteristics, and that, in the present state of Community law, is a matter for Member States'. The CJ added that such rules must comply with the principle of proportionality, a matter to be determined by the national court.

Note that post-*Keck*, this case would now be decided differently. National rules regulating trading hours on Sundays would be categorised as 'selling arrangements' and fall outside the scope of Art 34 TFEU altogether (*Punto Casa* [1994] and *Semeraro* [1996]).

■ Freedom of expression

In *Schmidberger* [2003], a protest by an environmental group which blocked an Austrian motorway was in breach of Art 34 TFEU. However, the CJ held that the restriction of free movement of goods was justified on grounds of freedom of expression and protection of fundamental rights. The demonstrators had sought permission from the Austrian authorities in advance and had only blocked the motorway for a limited amount of time, thus satisfying the proportionality requirement.

Proportionality
The requirements of proportionality (see below in the context of Art 36 TFEU) apply to the rule of reason. Many laws that might be justified, particularly on consumer protection grounds, are still found to be in breach of Art 36 TFEU because they are disproportionate (e.g. *Commission v Denmark*, considered above). Often the CJ suggests clear labelling as an alternative method of protecting public health and/or the interests of the consumer. This was the result in *Walter Rau v De Smedt* [1982], considered above.

In *Commission v Germany* [1987], German law provided that the name 'bier' could only be used for products brewed using malted barley, hops, yeast and water. The use of other ingredients, such as rice or maize, while not precluding the marketing of a product in Germany, meant that it could not be sold as 'bier'. The European Commission alleged that this law was in breach of Art 34 TFEU, because many imported beers did contain extra ingredients and thus could not be sold as 'bier'. The German government pleaded consumer protection. The CJ disagreed. While it was legitimate to seek to 'enable consumers who attribute specific qualities to beers manufactured from particular raw materials to make their choice in the light of that consideration', prohibiting the name 'bier' was excessive. The Court suggested that 'the compulsory affixing of suitable labels giving the nature of the product sold' would suffice instead.

In *Clinique* [1994], German legislation prohibited the sale of cosmetics under misleading names, designations or presentations by which certain properties could be ascribed to properties which they did not in fact have. The German authorities regarded the name *Clinique* as one such misleading name – it could mislead consumers into thinking the product had medicinal qualities, as it evoked associations with the word 'clinic'. The consequence of this was that the manufacturers, Estée Lauder, had to repackage their product for the German market (it was renamed *Linique*) and advertise it differently everywhere else, obviously increasing their costs greatly. Eventually they challenged the German authorities under Art 34 TFEU. The CJ agreed that the German legislation was capable of infringing Art 34 TFEU, but the German authorities responded with consumer protection. In the end, the Court held that the German rules were disproportionate: German consumers were sophisticated enough to appreciate that Clinique cosmetics did not have medicinal properties.

In *Commission v Spain and Italy* [2003], Italian and Spanish legislation banned the name 'chocolate' on packaging of chocolate products to which vegetable fats have been added. This affected British-made chocolate products, which traditionally contain vegetable fats. These could be sold in Italy and Spain only under the label 'chocolate substitute'. The European Commission launched actions on the basis that the legislation breached Art 34 TFEU because it forced chocolate producers in the UK (and some other Member States) to re-label their products for the Italian and Spanish markets. The Court agreed with the Commission. There was a breach of Art 34 TFEU because it was likely that Italian and Spanish consumers would regard products bearing the label 'chocolate substitute' as inferior, which would depress sales and thus restrict imports. The Court rejected Italy and Spain's defence of consumer protection. Although the Court acknowledged that it was important to draw consumers' attention to the fact that the chocolate products were not 'pure', this could be achieved by clearly indicating in the list of ingredients those vegetable fats that had been added.

Mutual recognition

In *Cassis de Dijon*, the CJ – as well as creating the rule of reason principle – established a presumption that, once goods have been 'lawfully produced and marketed in one of the Member States', they may be imported into any other State. This has become known as the principle of 'mutual recognition'. The presumption may only be rebutted by evidence that the goods in question pose a threat to one of the heads of Art 36 TFEU or one of the mandatory requirements.

The net result is to place the burden of proof on the authorities of the Member States seeking to justify their domestic legislation.

In practice, rebutting the presumption will not be easy to do. A successful rebuttal can be seen in *Müller* [1986]. French law restricted the use of E475, an emulsifying agent, in food. M, the manager of a baking company in France, had imported from Germany a cake and pastry mix called Phénix, which contained E475. He was prosecuted but claimed that the French law was in breach of Art 34 TFEU. The CJ agreed that the French law had the effect of restricting the importation of food from Germany, where the agent was freely available. However, the Court held that the law was justifiable under Art 36 TFEU on health grounds, taking into account the fact that consumption of bakery products was appreciably higher in France, particularly by children.

SUMMARY OF THE CASSIS DE DIJON JUDGMENT

The CJ confirmed that Art 34 TFEU (formerly Art 28 TEC) applies to indistinctly applicable rules which are non-discriminatory in nature.

The CJ accepted that Member States could justify such rules by invoking one (or more) of the mandatory requirements subject to the principle of proportionality ('rule of reason').

The CJ also introduced the principle of mutual recognition – once goods have been lawfully manufactured and marketed in one Member State, they can circulate freely in the common market unless a Member State can invoke a mandatory requirement or one of the derogations laid down in Art 36 TFEU (formerly Art 30 TEC).

SELLING ARRANGEMENTS

One problem with the *Dassonville* formula and its application to both distinctly and indistinctly applicable rules as noted by Weatherill and Beaumont (*EU Law*, 3rd edition, Penguin (1999)), is its failure to distinguish between national laws which impose a dual-burden on importers and those which impose an equal-burden on importers.

- **Dual-burden rules** are indistinctly applicable and apply to the content of goods, requiring the importer to comply with two sets of rules: the rules laid down in its own Member State, as well as the rules laid down in the

Member State into which the goods are being imported. These rules impose an additional burden on an importer, which can make the imported goods more costly and, therefore, hinder trade.

■ **Equal-burden rules** regulate trade and are indistinctly applicable (apply to both domestic producers and importers) but do not impose an additional burden on the importer. They are not protectionist in nature. They may have an impact on trade overall, but the burden is equal for all traders.

The CJ sought to deal with dual-burden rules in its *Cassis de Dijon* ruling with the introduction of the principle of mutual recognition and the 'rule of reason'.

> ▶ **CASSIS DE DIJON [1979]**
>
> German legislation laid down a minimum alcohol level of 25 per cent for cassis. Rewe-Zentrale, a German company, which sought to import French cassis with an alcohol level of approximately 20 per cent, argued that the German legislation contravened Art 34 TFEU. The German law created an additional burden (dual burden rule) for the importer, which hindered intra-State trade.
>
> The CJ held that if the product had been lawfully produced in accordance with French law then it could move freely in other Member States. It rejected the German Government's argument that the German legislation was necessary to protect consumers.

Post-*Cassis,* the CJ was required to rule on whether equal-burden rules were caught by Art 34 TFEU (formerly Art 28 TEC). More and more traders were exploiting the breadth of Art 34 TFEU to either challenge national measures, which were non-protectionist and non-discriminatory, or to raise Art 34 TFEU in their defence in proceedings brought against them for breach of national trading laws. The CJ's approach to such cases was inconsistent and created uncertainty. In some of its decisions, it ruled that equal-burden rules were outside the scope of Art 34 TFEU altogether: *Oebel* [1981]. In other cases, the CJ held that the national measures fell within the scope of Art 34 TFEU, but could be objectively justified in accordance with one of the mandatory requirements: *Cinetheque* [1985]; *Torfaen BC v B&Q plc* [1989]. The CJ attempted to resolve this uncertainty in 1993 in its judgment in *Keck and Mithouard* [1993].

In *Keck and Mithouard* [1993], K and M, two supermarket managers in France, were prosecuted under French law for re-selling (coffee and beer, respectively) lower than their purchase price. Such laws are designed to stop powerful companies from abusing their position and distorting the market by undercutting smaller rivals. K and M argued that French law hindered EU trade. The CJ began by citing *Dassonville*, and acknowledged that the French law in question 'may restrict the volume of sales . . . insofar as it deprives traders of a method of sales promotion'. However, in view of the increasing tendency of traders to seek to avoid non-protectionist national laws by relying on Art 34 TFEU, the CJ decided to review its position. It concluded that:

'. . . contrary to what has previously been decided, the application to products . . . of national provisions restricting or prohibiting certain selling arrangements is not such as to hinder, directly or indirectly, actually or potentially, trade between Member States within the meaning of the *Dassonville* judgment, so long as they affect in the same manner, in law and in fact, the marketing of domestic products and of those from other Member States. Where these conditions are fulfilled, the application of such rules to the sale of products from another Member State meeting the requirements laid down by that State is not by nature such as to prevent their access to the market or to impede access any more than it impedes the access of domestic products. Such rules therefore fall outside the scope of Art [36 TFEU] (formerly Art 28 TEC).' (Para 16.)

The result of the decision in *Keck and Mithouard* is that it is now necessary to draw a distinction between two categories of national law when assessing whether or not Art 34 TFEU has been infringed:

- 'Certain selling arrangements' – if a national law concerns when and/or how goods are sold, it may be regarded as 'selling arrangements' and is not MEQRs within the scope of Art 34 TFEU altogether provided it applies equally to all traders in law and in fact.
- Laws relating to the characteristics of a product, such as weights and measures, packaging, ingredients, etc. are regarded as 'product

> requirements' and are MEQRs. They are, therefore, prohibited by
> Art 34 TFEU (*Dassonville* applies), unless justified under Art 36 TFEU
> or the *Cassis* mandatory requirements.

This new approach has been confirmed in a variety of cases since 1993. It is also possible to look back over the CJ's pre-1993 case law and identify a number of cases that would be decided differently now: contrast *Torfaen BC v B&Q plc* [1989] with *Punto Casa* [1994] and *Semeraro* [1996]. This is why, in *Keck and Mithouard*, the Court used the phrase 'contrary to what has previously been decided' at the start of para 16 of its judgment. It is now possible to identify a variety of national laws that will be classified as 'selling arrangements'.

▶ KECK AND MITHOUARD [1993]

Two supermarket managers were prosecuted for re-selling coffee and beer for lower than their purchase price. This was an offence under French law, but the managers claimed that the law was contrary to Art 34 TFEU, which prohibits measures having an equivalent effect to quantitative restrictions on imports.

In a landmark judgment, the CJ did a rare U-turn and held that the French law related to 'selling arrangements' and applied equally to all traders in law and in fact and was, therefore, outside the scope of Art 34 TFEU.

In *Tankstation t'Heukske & JBE Boermans* [1994], Dutch legislation required all shops to close during the night (subject to certain limited exceptions, e.g. petrol stations). Two Dutch traders were prosecuted and convicted for breaching this rule. On appeal, they argued that the Dutch rules imposed a restriction on intra-State trade. The CJ disagreed; following *Keck and Mithouard*, the Dutch rules simply constituted a selling arrangement.

Commission v Greece [1995] involved Greek legislation imposing a requirement that powdered milk for infants was only to be sold in pharmacists' shops. In *Banchero* [1996], Italian law reserved the sale of tobacco products to authorised retail outlets only. Both national rules were held to be selling arrangements.

Further problems have arisen in the case law concerning the meaning of 'selling arrangements' and, in particular, the application of the *Keck* ruling to advertising rules. In both *Hünermund* [1993] – German law banning pharmacists from advertising on the radio, on TV or at the cinema – and *Leclerc-Siplec* [1995] – French law prohibiting television advertising in the distribution sector – the CJ ruled that Art 34 TFEU did not apply. In the latter case, Advocate-General Jacobs criticised the CJ's approach in *Keck* on the ground that advertising could play an important role in breaking down barriers to trade between Member States and increasing market access. He suggested a modification to the *Keck* formula by inserting a *de minimis* threshold – a selling arrangement which was non-discriminatory would fall within Art 34 TFEU if it had a substantial impact on trade. The CJ did not follow the Advocate-General's approach in *Leclerc-Siplec*, but it has been suggested by Craig and de Búrca that his market access argument influenced the Court in *De Agostini* and *Gourmet Internationale* (in which he was also the Advocate-General), which are discussed below.

In two cases, concerning a total ban in advertising, the CJ held that Art 34 TFEU did apply. *De Agostini* [1997] concerned the legality of advertising laws in Sweden, which prohibited advertising designed to attract the attention of children under 12. The CJ was of the view that the advertising ban may not satisfy the *Keck* test in its entirety. It accepted that the advertising rules may amount to a selling arrangement and fall outside the scope of Art 34 TFEU, but it was not clear whether the ban applied equally to all traders in law and in fact. It held that, 'It cannot be excluded that an outright ban, applying in one Member State, of a type of promotion for a product which is lawfully sold there might have a greater impact on products from other Member States' (para 42). It was for the national court to determine whether the second limb of the *Keck* test had been satisfied and whether the national law could be justified under Art 36 TFEU or one of the *Cassis* mandatory requirements.

In another case, the Court decided that another Swedish advertising law, effectively prohibiting any advertising of alcohol, did infringe Art 34 TFEU. In *Gourmet Internationale Products* [2001], the CJ found that this was likely to have a greater impact on imported alcoholic products than on Swedish alcoholic products, with which Swedish consumers were more familiar. The Court held:

'. . . a prohibition of all advertising . . . is liable to impede access to the market by products from other Member States more than it impedes access by domestic products, with which consumers are instantly more familiar . . . A prohibition on advertising . . . must therefore be regarded as affecting the marketing of products from other Member States more heavily than the marketing of domestic products and as therefore constituting an obstacle to trade between Member States . . .'

Keck broadly reflects an inequality-based understanding of Art 34 TFEU and it is thus surprising that the court in *Alfa Vita* [2006] ruled that the measure concerned was neither to be unequal in effect nor to prevent access completely but merely to reduce sales (see Chalmers, Davies and Monti, *European Union Law*, 2nd edn, Cambridge University Press (2010), p 775). Even though *Keck* and *Alfa Vita* apply to different categories of measures so that there is no hard conflict, there is a conceptual inconsistency as to the fact that the idea of MEQR underlying the law of selling arrangements is not the same as that underlying the law on other types of MEQR.

SUMMARY OF *KECK AND MITHOUARD*

An indistinctly applicable rule which may be categorised as a selling arrangement will fall outside the scope of Art 34 TFEU altogether provided that it applies equally to all traders in law and in fact.

If the national measure does not apply equally in law and in fact to all traders, it will infringe Art 34 TFEU unless it can be justified in accordance with one of the derogations laid down in Art 36 TFEU or one of the *Cassis de Dijon* mandatory requirements.

DEROGATION FROM ARTS 34 AND 35: ART 36 TFEU (FORMERLY ARTS 28 AND 29: ART 30 TEC)

The drafters of the EC Treaty recognised that many national laws might have the effect of preventing imports but that there might be overriding reasons why the national law should prevail over EU law. Hence, Art 36 TFEU (formerly Art 30 TEC) provides that certain national laws may be justified on various grounds.

Art 36 TFEU provides:

The provisions of Arts 34 and 35 shall not preclude prohibitions or restrictions on imports, exports or goods in transit justified on grounds of public morality, public policy or public security; the protection of health and life of humans, animals or plants; the protection of national treasures possessing artistic, historic or archaeological value; or the protection of industrial or commercial property. Such prohibitions or restrictions shall not, however, constitute a means of arbitrary discrimination or a disguised restriction on trade between Member States.

The grounds listed are exhaustive and may not be added to (*Commission v Italy* [1982]). Moreover, the grounds have been restrictively interpreted, because they operate as exceptions to the fundamental principle, that of the free movement of goods.

The grounds under Art 36 TFEU

Public morality

Public morality is something for Member States to decide in accordance with their own values. This principle was established in *R v Henn and Darby* [1979] in order to secure central values of a society. The defendants had imported a consignment of pornographic films and magazines into the UK from Denmark. Most of the films and magazines were lawfully produced and marketed in Denmark. However, the consignment was detected by British customs at Felixstowe and the defendants were arrested. They were jointly convicted of being 'knowingly concerned in the fraudulent evasion of the prohibition of the importation of obscene articles', under the UK's Customs Consolidation Act 1876. On appeal, they argued that Art 34 TFEU provided a defence, while the prosecution invoked Art 36 TFEU to justify the UK customs legislation. The Court of Appeal rejected their appeal but, on further appeal to the House of Lords, a reference was made to the CJ. The Court held that the 1876 Act was subject to Art 34 TFEU but was justifiable under Art 36 TFEU. The measure was genuinely applied for the protection of British public morality. The morality exception merely concerns free movement of goods, so where morality questions arise in other fields they are treated as public policy matters.

Public policy

Despite potential width, this has rarely been successfully invoked. However, in *R v Thompson* [1978], a restriction on the exportation of silver coins from the

UK was justified on public policy grounds, since the State had an interest in protecting its mint coinage.

Public security
This ground is also rarely pleaded successfully in defence of national laws. One such case was *Campus Oil* [1982]. Irish law required importers of petroleum oils to buy 35 per cent of their petrol from the Irish National Petroleum Company, at fixed prices. Although the law was discriminatory, and protective, it was held to be justified. The law was necessary to maintain a viable refinery in Ireland that could meet the nation's essential needs in the event of a crisis. Supplies of petroleum for fuel and other uses was of fundamental importance to a country's existence, since it was needed not only for the economy, but for its inhabitants, including the emergency services.

Protection of the health and life of humans, animals and plants
This ground has, unsurprisingly, been utilised to try to justify many national rules and measures. It has, however, been held that there must be a 'real health risk'. This will not be the case if the exporting State maintains equivalent standards. In *Commission v UK* [1983], UK law required that ultra heat-treated milk be marketed by approved dairies only – allegedly to ensure milk was free from bacterial infection – which necessitated the reheating and repackaging of imported milk. This law was held to be unjustified. Nor was an import licence justified. There was evidence that imported milk was of similar quality, and subject to the same standards, as UK milk.

There must also be a 'seriously considered health policy' in the State seeking to restrict imports. In *Commission v UK* [1982], the UK government announced a prohibition on the importation of poultry meat and eggs from all Member States except Ireland and Denmark. The ostensible aim of the prohibition was to prevent the spread of 'Newcastle disease' by only allowing imports from those States (i.e. Ireland and Denmark), with a slaughtering policy in the event of an outbreak of the disease. The CJ found that the prohibition was unjustified, on the ground that there was no 'seriously considered health policy'. There had been little in the way of research, reports or studies. Rather, there was evidence showing that the prohibition followed domestic pressure to restrict growing imports of French poultry, especially as it was timed to coincide with Christmas and thus prevent the sale of French turkeys in the UK.

The majority of cases involve imports of food and drink, but Art 36 TFEU has wider scope than that. In *Toolex Alpha* [2000], Swedish law prohibited the sale and use of chemical products composed wholly or partially of a chemical called trichloroethylene (TE). According to the Swedish government, the chemical was carcinogenic, that is, it posed a risk of cancer in humans as well as posing a threat to the environment. Toolex Alpha, a manufacturer of machine parts used in the production of CDs, used TE to remove residues of grease produced during the manufacturing process. They challenged the Swedish rules, alleging a breach of Art 34 TFEU. The Swedish government successfully relied upon Art 36 TFEU.

The CJ in *Greenham & Abel* [2004] issued important new guidelines on the scope of the health derogation, particularly designed for use in cases where products are not universally banned throughout the EU but are only banned in certain states. The case involved French legislation prohibiting the sale of adulterated food. Under the legislation, certain substances were banned (including a chemical substance called Q10). Two men had been charged with selling a product called 'Juice Plus', to which Q10 had been added. The men claimed that Q10 had been in free circulation in Spain and Italy since 1995 and in Germany and the UK since 2000. They, therefore, maintained that the French prohibition of Q10 breached Article 34 TFEU. The CJ responded that national rules restricting imports where justification is sought on health grounds 'must be based on a detailed assessment of the risk to public health, based on the most reliable scientific data available and the most recent results of international research'. Whether the rules were, in fact, justified was a question for the national courts.

Protection of national treasures
For example, a national law preventing art treasures leaving a country might be justified (see *Commission v Italy* [1968]). This ground would probably only apply to exports.

Protection of industrial and commercial property
This covers intellectual property rights (copyright, trade marks and patents), and is beyond the scope of this book.

'Arbitrary' discrimination
Even if a measure is covered by Art 36 TFEU, it will still be unlawful if it amounts to 'arbitrary' discrimination. In *Conegate Ltd* [1986], a British

company had imported inflatable rubber dolls into the UK from Germany. A number of consignments of dolls and other sex articles were seized at Gatwick Airport by HM customs officers under the Customs Consolidation Act 1876 (the same legislation as in *R v Henn and Darby* [1979]). The company brought an action for recovery of the dolls, relying on Art 34 TFEU. The customs authorities relied on Art 36 TFEU. However, the CJ held that Art 36 TFEU did not apply because, although the sale of such products was restricted in the UK (to licensed sex shops and mail order outlets), it was not banned. Therefore, to refuse importation of the German dolls, when practically identical products were on sale in the UK, would constitute arbitrary discrimination.

A 'disguised restriction on trade'

A national law that would otherwise be protected by Art 36 TFEU may be castigated as a disguised restriction on trade. An example would be the import ban on French poultry in *Commission v UK* [1982], above.

Proportionality

The grounds of exemption under Article 36 TFEU appear generous. However, the CJ has consistently held that the purpose of the Article is to allow certain national laws and rules to derogate from the free movement provisions only to the extent to which they are 'justified' in order to achieve the objectives in the Article. A measure may be justified provided it does what is necessary to achieve the objectives in the first sentence of Art 36, and further that it does no more than necessary. If there are other methods capable of achieving that objective which are less restrictive of intra-EU trade, then they should be used instead. In *De Peijper* [1976], for example, the CJ said:

> ... national rules or practices which do restrict imports ... or are capable of doing so are only compatible with the Treaty to the extent to which they are *necessary* ... National rules or practices do not fall within the exemptions specified in [Art 36 TFEU] if [their objectives] can as effectively be protected by measures which do not restrict intra-Community trade so much.

Relationship between Art 36 TFEU and harmonising directives

Where harmonising directives in a particular area have been adopted, Member States may not unilaterally adopt, on their own authority, corrective or protective measures designed to obviate any breach by another Member State of

EU law. In *Hedley Lomas* [1996] – discussed in Chapter 2 – the CJ held that recourse to Art 36 TFEU (on grounds of protection of animal health) was not possible because of the presence of Directive 74/577 regulating conditions in slaughterhouses throughout the EU.

CHECKLIST FOR APPLICATION OF ARTICLE 34 TFEU (FORMERLY ARTICLE 28 TEC)

- Is the national measure at issue a 'State measure'? If the hindrance in trade results from the actions of private parties, could *Commission v. France* or *Schmidberger* apply?
- If it is, is it a QR? If so, Art 36 TFEU may apply.
- Is it a distinctly or an indistinctly applicable measure?
- If it is a distinctly applicable measure, apply *Dassonville*. If it has a restrictive effect on trade, it is in breach of Art 34 TFEU unless justified under Art 36 TFEU or a mandatory requirement subject to the principle of proportionality.
- If it is an indistinctly applicable measure, is it a selling arrangement or does it relate to the characteristics of the product?
- If it is a selling arrangement, it will fall outside the scope of Art 34 TFEU in accordance with *Keck*, provided it applies equally to all traders in law and in fact. If it does not, it may be justified under Art 36 TFEU or a mandatory requirement subject to the principle of proportionality.
- If it is a rule relating to the characteristic of a product, it may be a MEQR, unless it can be justified under Art 36 TFEU or a mandatory requirement subject to the principle of proportionality.

You should now be confident that you would be able to tick all of the boxes on the checklist at the beginning of this chapter. To check your knowledge of Free movement of goods why not visit the companion website and take the Multiple Choice Question test. Check your understanding of the terms and vocabulary used in this chapter with the flashcard glossary.

8

Putting it into practice . . .

Now that you've mastered the basics, you will want to put it all into practice. The Routledge Questions and Answers series provides an ideal opportunity for you to apply your understanding and knowledge of the law and to hone your essay-writing technique.

We've included one exam-style essay question, which replicates the type of question posed in the Routledge Questions and Answers series, to give you some essential exam practice. The Q&A includes an answer plan and a fully worked model answer to help you recognise what examiners might look for in your answer.

QUESTION 1

Discuss the extent to which the principle of direct effect effectively protects individuals' EU rights before their national courts.

Answer plan

Direct effect is a very popular topic on exam papers as either an essay or problem question. Essay questions often require you to demonstrate an understanding of the development of the concept by the CJ through its case law, its limitations and the alternative mechanisms of enforcement developed by the CJ for individuals whose EU rights have been infringed. The main points to be covered in your answer to the question set out above are:

- origin and development of the principle of direct effect by the CJ;
- limitations of the principle of direct effect, particularly the prohibition on the horizontal direct effect of directives, the implications of this prohibition and its relationship with the principle of incidental horizontal direct effect;
- alternatives developed by the CJ – broad interpretation of the State, principle of indirect effect and State liability.

ANSWER

The principle of direct effect was introduced by the CJ in its seminal judgment in *Van Gend en Loos* in 1963. The Court adopted a teleological interpretation of the original EC Treaty and held that it had created a 'new legal order', which created rights for individuals as well as for the Member States which had become part of their legal heritage. The principle of direct effect enables individuals to enforce rights conferred on them by EU law directly before their national courts. However, not all provisions of EU law have direct effect. In *Van Gend en Loos*, the CJ set out a test of 'justiciability'. It was summarised by AG Mayras in *Reyners* as follows: 'A provision must be sufficiently clear and precise, unconditional and "complete and legally perfect" in order to be relied on before a national court.' In *Van Gend en Loos*, the CJ held that Art 12 TEC (now Art 30 TFEU and formerly Art 25 TEC), a negative obligation, which prohibits Member States from introducing new customs duties on imported goods from other Member States, produces direct effects. In *Lütticke*, the concept was extended to include positive obligations where the time limit for implementation has expired. In *Defrenne (No 2)*, the CJ held that Treaty provisions could have horizontal as well as vertical direct effect. In other words, they could be relied upon in actions against other individuals as well as against the State.

The principle of direct effect fills an important gap in the original EC Treaty which provided limited means of redress for individuals who had had their EU rights infringed (Arts 263, 265 and 340 TFEU (formerly Arts 230, 232 and 288 TEC)) and complements the public enforcement mechanism set out in Art 258 TFEU (formerly Art 226 TEC), which enables the Commission to bring an action against a Member State that has infringed EU law.

The CJ enhanced the protection of individuals' EU rights further by extending direct effect to include regulations (*Politi*), decisions (*Grad*) and directives (*Van Duyn*). Its extension to directives in *Van Duyn* was an important, yet controversial development. It was thought that directives did not satisfy the test for direct effect as they require implementation by the Member State. However, the CJ held that the *effet utile* of a directive would be undermined if an individual could not rely on its provisions before a national court. Further, in *Ratti*, the CJ added that a Member State should not be allowed to prevent an individual from relying on their EU rights because of the State's own failure to implement the directive correctly or on time (estoppel argument). It also added that a directive cannot have direct effect until the date for implementation has passed.

Some of the Member States were hostile to the extension of direct effect to directives, particularly Germany and France. It has been suggested that in response to this criticism, the CJ limited the scope of the direct effect of directives in its *Marshall (No 1)* judgment. In this case, the CJ made a distinction between vertical and horizontal direct effect of directives. It held that directives can only be invoked by a private party against the State (vertical direct effect) and not against another private party (horizontal direct effect). The reasons given by the CJ were that since directives were addressed to Member States only under Article 288 TFEU (formerly Article 249 TEC), they cannot confer rights and obligations directly on individuals which can be invoked *inter se*.

This distinction between vertical and horizontal direct effect of directives has several disadvantages. First, the full effectiveness of directives is undermined. Second, the uniform application of EU law is restricted and finally, it places an individual at a disadvantage if seeking to enforce their rights against another private party. This has created a gap in the protection of rights conferred on individuals in the field of employment and consumer protection. For example, in *Duke v GEC Reliance Ltd* [1988], the employee of a private company was unable to rely on the Equal Treatment Directive against her employer. This was in marked contrast to the case of *Marshall (No 1)*, where the claimant was able to rely on the same directive in similar circumstances because her employer was a Health Authority and construed to be an 'emanation of the State'.

Yet, despite this difference in protection between public and private sector workers, the CJ had refused on two further occasions to reverse its ruling in *Marshall (No 1)* and recognise horizontal direct effect of directives (*Faccini Dori* in 1990 and *Pfeiffer* in 2005). The CJ emphasised that to recognise horizontal direct effect of directives would blur the distinction between regulations and directives laid down in Article 288 TFEU (formerly Art 249 TEC). In other words, the EU only has competence to enact Regulations which may impose rights and obligations on individuals, but not directives.

In its *CIA* ruling, it was thought that the CJ had reversed its prohibition of horizontal direct effect of directives. This case involved a dispute between two private parties. CIA had brought an action against the defendants arguing that it had been libelled by their claim that its product (an alarm system) had not been approved by Belgian law. CIA claimed that the Belgian law at issue was unenforceable as it had not been notified to the Commission in accordance with Directive 89/189. On referral to the CJ under Article 267 TFEU (formerly Article 234 TEC), the CJ held that the relevant provision of the directive was directly effective and that the Belgian law was in breach of Union law. The impact of the ruling was to allow CIA to rely on the directive in its defence against an action brought by another private party and led to suggestions that the CJ had overruled its position in *Marshall (No 1)* and *Faccini Dori*. The CJ took the opportunity to clarify this development in the subsequent case of *Unilever*. It confirmed that its ruling in *Faccini Dori* was still good law and that a directive cannot of itself impose obligations on individuals. However, it distinguished the situation in *Unilever* and held that in such limited circumstances, the orthodox rule does not apply. The Directive at issue in this case (and in *CIA*) does not create rights or obligations for individuals. The main aim of Directive 89/189 is to promote free movement of goods by introducing a preventative control mechanism. Breach of this directive renders national technical regulations inapplicable, even in civil proceedings between two private parties concerning contractual rights and obligations.

The CJ has developed alternative mechanisms for protecting the rights of private parties before their national courts, namely the adoption of a broad interpretation of the 'State', the principle of indirect effect and the principle of State liability.

In *Marshall (No 1)* itself, the CJ adopted a broad interpretation of the 'State' which enabled the applicant to successfully rely on the provisions of the Equal Treatment Directive in a claim for discriminatory dismissal against her employer, a Health Authority. The latter was deemed to be an 'emanation of the State'. In *Foster*, it ruled that a State entity which provides public services under the (indirect) control of the State and which has been conferred 'special powers' in order to carry out this task may be considered to be an emanation of the State.

A second mechanism for individuals to effectively enforce their EU rights is the principle of indirect effect. In *Von Colson*, on the basis of Art 4 TEU (formerly Art 10 TEC), the CJ imposed a duty on national courts to interpret national law to comply with Union law as far as it is possible to do so. This obligation arises from the date the measure comes into force (*Adeneler*), although prior to this, a Member State must avoid introducing measures which could conflict with the objective of a directive (*Inter-Environnement Wallonie ASBL*).

The main advantage of the principle of indirect effect is that it avoids the test for direct effect (as in *Von Colson*) and has been applied in disputes between private parties (*Marleasing*). Yet, whilst the scope of the obligation is broad (it applies to all national law, including pre-existing national law), the CJ has recognised certain limits to the application of the principle of indirect effect by national courts. It does not require national courts to interpret national law *contra legem* (*Wagner Miret*), nor where an interpretation would conflict with the principles of legal certainty and non-retroactivity, particularly in criminal matters (*Kolpinghuis*, *Arcaro*).

Where the principles of direct effect and indirect effect are not applicable, individuals may be able to bring an action for damages against a Member State for breach of EU law. The principle of State liability was introduced by the CJ in its *Francovich* case in 1991. Italy had failed to implement a directive by the prescribed date, depriving employees of their right to payment of arrears in salary arising from the insolvency of their employer. The CJ held that a Member State was required to pay compensation for the losses sustained by the applicants arising from non-implementation of the directive provided the following three conditions were satisfied: the provision conferred rights on individuals; these rights were identifiable from the directive itself; a causal link could be found between the breach of the provision and the losses sustained. In the later case of *Factortame (No 3)* and *Brasserie du Pêcheur*, the CJ amended the test which now requires the provision in question to confer rights on individuals, the breach to be sufficiently serious and there to be a causal link between the breach and the loss sustained. In assessing whether or not the breach is sufficiently serious, there must be a manifest and grave disregard of any limits on the discretion of the Member State. The national court should take into account the following factors in making this assessment: clarity and precision of the rule breached; the measure of discretion left to the Member State/Union; whether the infringement was voluntary or involuntary; whether any error of law was excusable or non-excusable; whether a Union institution may have contributed to the breach; the adoption and retention of measures contrary to Union law.

It is significant that the principle of State liability is a EU remedy common to all the Member States and is independent of the principles of direct effect and indirect effect. Nevertheless, the principle of State liability is not a panacea for protecting individuals' rights. Damages may only be awarded if the breach is sufficiently serious.

The CJ has sought to create a system of effective judicial protection for individuals seeking to enforce their EU rights directly before their national courts. The principle of direct effect is the fundamental pillar of this system. However, its impact is undermined by the lack of horizontal direct effect of directives. Despite examining the issue on two further occasions, the CJ has not reversed its ruling in *Marshall (No 1)*. However, to mitigate the consequences of its prohibition, the CJ has developed a number of innovative alternatives, such as adopting a broad interpretation of what constitutes the 'State', the principle of indirect effect and the principle of State liability, which have all extended the possibilities available to individuals wishing to enforce their EU law rights before their national courts.

Each Routledge Q&A contains fifty essay and problem-based questions on topics commonly found on exam papers, complete with answer plans and fully worked model answers. For further examination practice, visit the Routledge website or your local bookstore today!